LOVE YOUR LUNCHBOX

JAMES RAMSDEN

do-ahead recipes to liven up lunchtime

CONTENTS

INTRODUCTION

For many children of my generation, the lunchbox was a treasured possession. My Thomas the Tank Engine one was so cool that my five-year-old self practically paraded down the street to school; its contents, whatever they were, however similar to yesterday's pickings, offered fresh promise, new excitements, and something to look forward to at midday. Would it be a cheese and pickle sandwich or a ham and lettuce bap? Would there be a chocolate biscuit or a fruit roll-up? Capri Sun or Um Bongo? Golden Delicious (thumbs up) or Granny Smith (thumbs down)? The intrigue!

With this book I want to re-inject that sense of potential, that sense of anticipation, that frisson of a well-whetted appetite to the often-too-ordinary midweek lunch. But for grown-ups. Why should kids get all the fun while the grown-ups eat the same lunch in front of their computers each day? Why not follow the Japanese and dive head first into a steaming bowl of slippery noodles, or the New Yorkers with their pastrami and rye bread, or our Mediterranean cousins with their fresh salads and nourishing grains? These lunches are resourceful, creative and practical. But in every case, it is flavour that comes first, with convenience a happy corollary and not the other way round.

Of course, moveable lunches needn't be restricted to the office – many of the dishes here will be just as happy on a beach, up a mountain, by a river, or in the park. Wherever you find yourself unwrapping your lunch, I want it to have all the delight of a Christmas stocking, and none of the disappointment. We don't want the same sandwich every day any more than we want the same pair of socks every Christmas.

Love Your Lunchbox is a book for anyone who wants better socks. Or, rather, lunch. For anyone for whom lunch is something to enjoy rather than endure, to linger over rather than bolt down, to make yourself rather than make yourself walk to the shops in the rain for. If that sounds like you, then you're in the right place.

This book is about the spirit of the lunchbox, rather than the vessel itself. A trend for vintage lunchboxes would be a happy thing (there's no shortage online), though a Tupperware and a carrier bag will do the trick. As mother always told me, it's what's on the inside that counts.

COOKING

These recipes are written to be prepared and cooked in advance and eaten later that day, or the following couple of days. Some of them are doable in a matter of minutes on the morning you plan to eat them, others may require a bit of time the evening before. This isn't necessarily a book for every day. Instead, it's for those evenings when you find you have a slice of time to prepare a lunch or two, or a Sunday afternoon to put a few bits in the freezer.

REHEATING AND EATING

Although these dishes are intended to be made in advance, clearly there is nothing stopping you devouring the thing on the spot. It would, however, get a little repetitive of me to say 'eat now or chill for later' on each recipe, so you can assume this is the case with all the recipes unless otherwise stated.

You will generally need a toaster, a microwave, or a kettle to finish those recipes that can't be eaten cold.

ON MICROWAVING

Ignore the baseless claims about microwaves 'nuking' nutrients and embrace their incredibly efficient means of heating up, and indeed cooking, food. Generally dishes should be covered with clingfilm to reheat, if only to minimize spattering, with a few holes poked in the clingfilm. Avoid putting any metal, including foil, in the microwave.

SERVINGS

Most of the recipes in this book serve two, meaning you can either lovingly prepare lunch for yourself and your other half, or lovingly prepare lunch for yourself for the next two days, or lovingly prepare yourself a single lunch of quite unnecessarily large proportions.

COST

Each recipe aims for a cost of less than £5 a head (often considerably less). At the time of writing, the average cost of lunch for an office worker is reported to be £7.81, so less than a fiver seems about right for a homemade lunch that leaves you with a few quid for a Coca Cola/Snickers fix.

A caveat: I don't know what's in your fridge or cupboard. There will be recipes in this book that cost you a little more to shop for, but that's because you may need to buy, say, rice vinegar, or a spice of which you'll use only a tablespoon. In all these cases, I've done my best to make sure such items are not perishable, and can be used and reused. Those that aren't can be frozen.

ONE LAST THOUGHT...

There has been some debate recently about the relative merits or otherwise of eating lunch at your desk, with a health minister labelling the practice 'disgusting'. I say it's entirely up to you where you strap on the nosebag, though perhaps be aware that some colleagues might object to a particularly pungent curry distracting them from crucial research on the *Daily Mail* website.

CHAPTER 1
WEEKEND LOOSE ENDS

This chapter presupposes that you will cook certain things over the weekend.
And when I say weekend, I mostly mean Sunday lunch. Your weekend may follow
many paths. There might be a bowl of pasta on Friday night, curry on Saturday,
a breakfast somewhere along the way, perhaps involving muffins and croissants
and bacon. An entire day might be lost to pints and pork scratchings,
or to prams and tantrums and takeaway pizza.

But Sundays, on the whole, are more predictable. Sundays are for a roast.
Pork belly or roast chicken or a rib of beef. There will be roast potatoes, which I've
yet to fashion into anything decent the following day, and so are absent from this
chapter, though roast root vegetables (p.10) are always very fine and very adaptable.

And, after all, Sunday is the plum day for preparing a couple of lunches
for the week ahead.

BEEF AND POTATO PASTY

Ne'er was there a morsel so fraught with controversy. Devon or Cornwall? Side crimp or top crimp? Swede or no swede? These are all very important questions, but as long as the thing tastes good, I couldn't give a stuff.

Now, I'm all in favour of making your own pastry, but in this case – by which I mean the case of making your lunch – it may be a little too much to ask.

Prep time: 20 minutes
Cooking time: 30–40 minutes, plus chilling
Freezable? Yes

300g/10^1/$_2$oz shortcrust pastry
20g/^{3}/$_4$oz/1^1/$_2$ tbsp butter
1 onion, peeled and chopped
salt and pepper
1 tsp chopped thyme
2 tbsp chopped parsley
125–150g/4^1/$_2$–5^1/$_2$oz leftover beef, chopped
100g/3^1/$_2$oz cooked potato, cubed
100g/3^1/$_2$oz cooked swede (optional: use potato
    instead if preferred), cubed
1 egg, beaten

AT HOME

Preheat the oven to 180°C/350°F/Gas mark 4. Divide the pastry in two and roll out to about 5mm/^{1}/$_4$in thick, then cut out two rounds, each about 20cm/8in in diameter. Chill.

Melt the butter in a saucepan over a medium-low heat and add the onion. Season with salt and pepper, and cook until soft, stirring occasionally. Add the herbs, beef, potato and swede, if using. Give it a good mix. Taste for seasoning and leave to cool.

Top each pastry with the filling and fold over. Crimp to seal, then brush with the beaten egg. Prick a couple of times to let the air out, then bake for 20–25 minutes, until golden brown. Cool, cover and store in the fridge for up to 2 days.

IN EACH LUNCHBOX

A pasty.

TO FINISH

Reheat (if you wish) in an oven at 180°C/350°F/Gas mark 4 for 10 minutes. A microwave will heat it, but will also make it a little soggy.

Roast vegetables with lentils, chilli and feta

The temptation with leftover roast vegetables – by which I mean any or all of: beetroot, celeriac, butternut squash, parsnip, red onion (always), garlic (ditto), swede, turnip, and so on – is to boil them briefly with stock and blend them into a soup. It's a temptation worth submitting to every now and then, creating a rich and deeply flavoured soup. But for something a little lighter and more textural, this salady number is a winner.

If you fancy making it from scratch, veg and all, then cut root veg into 2.5cm/1in cubes, toss with olive oil, salt, pepper and unpeeled garlic cloves, and roast at 200°C/400°F/Gas mark 6 for 45 minutes to 1 hour.

Prep time: 10 minutes
Cooking time: 20 minutes
Freezable? No

85g/3oz/scant ½ cup green lentils
400g/14oz roasted vegetables
a good handful of rocket (arugula)
85g/3oz feta cheese, lightly crumbled
salt and pepper

For the dressing
1 red chilli, deseeded and finely chopped
a good squeeze of lemon
4 tbsp olive oil
a handful of parsley, finely chopped

AT HOME

Rinse the lentils under running water, then cook according to packet instructions. Drain and rinse under cold water to prevent overcooking. Shake until dry.

Toss together the roasted vegetables, lentils, rocket and feta. Season with salt and plenty of pepper, and store in the fridge for up to 2 days.

To make the dressing, mix together the chilli, lemon juice, oil and parsley. Season with salt and pepper. Taste and adjust with more lemon, olive oil or salt as necessary. Store in a small pot in the fridge.

IN EACH LUNCHBOX

Portion of roast vegetable and lentil salad; portion of dressing.

TO FINISH

Dress before serving.

CAESAR SALAD

I was as disappointed, as no doubt you will be, to discover that this salad was not invented by the great warrior, dictator and leader of the Roman Empire Julius Caesar, but an Italian–American chap called Caesar Cardini. This excellent salad pales somewhat when you realize it wasn't concocted between invasions of Britain and bloody encounters with Gauls. But no matter. It's still a superb dish and dead easy to chuck together.

   This is something of a base recipe. By all means gussy it up with whatever bits and pieces you fancy – bacon, tomatoes, squirrel…

Prep time: 15 minutes

Cooking time: 5 minutes

Freezable? No

2 tsp olive oil

a sprig of rosemary

a few small chunks of bread

crisp lettuce leaves, such as romaine, cos
      or little gem

150g/5^{1}/2oz roast chicken, shredded

10 anchovy fillets (optional)

For the dressing

1 egg yolk

1 tsp Dijon mustard

100ml/3^{1}/2fl oz/scant ^{1}/2 cup olive oil

1 small garlic clove, peeled and crushed to a paste

15g/^{1}/2oz grated Parmesan cheese

juice of ^{1}/2 lemon

a few shakes of Tabasco sauce

salt and pepper

AT HOME

Heat the oil and rosemary in a frying pan over a medium heat, add the bread and fry, tossing occasionally, until golden and crisp. Drain the croutons on kitchen paper, discarding the rosemary.

   Wash and dry the salad leaves if necessary, then assemble with the chicken, croutons, and the anchovies, if using. Cover and store in the fridge for up to 24 hours.

   To make the dressing, whisk together the egg yolk and mustard, then very slowly add the oil, whisking continuously to emulsify. Add the garlic, Parmesan, lemon juice and Tabasco, and season with salt and pepper. Store in a jar in the fridge.

IN EACH LUNCHBOX

Portion of salad; portion of dressing.

TO FINISH

Dress the salad and eat.

NORTH AFRICAN–STYLE
CHICKEN BROTH

In truth, you could do this with any leftover meat. Lamb or beef will benefit from a longer, gentler cooking time.

Ras-el-hanout is a North African spice blend that you can find in the spice section of most supermarkets these days.

Prep time: 15 minutes
Cooking time: 20 minutes
Freezable? Yes

olive oil
1 small onion, peeled and finely chopped
1 garlic clove, peeled and finely chopped
salt and pepper
2 tsp ras-el-hanout
1/2 tsp chilli flakes
400g/14oz canned chopped tomatoes
400ml/14fl oz/1 2/3 cups chicken stock
a pinch of sugar
50g/1 3/4oz/5 tbsp couscous
70–100g/2 1/2–3 1/2oz cooked chicken, shredded
2 preserved lemons, flesh discarded, peel roughly
    chopped (optional)

AT HOME
Heat a splash of oil in a saucepan over a low heat and add the onion and garlic. Season with salt and pepper, cover and cook for 10 minutes, stirring occasionally, until soft.

Turn up the heat to medium and add the spices. Stir briefly, then add the tomatoes, stock, and a pinch of sugar. Simmer for 7–10 minutes.

Meanwhile, boil a kettle and cook the couscous according to packet instructions.

Stir the cooked couscous and shredded chicken through the soup. If using, add the chopped lemon. Cool, cover, and store in the fridge for up to 2 days.

IN EACH LUNCHBOX
A portion of broth (in a microwaveable container).

TO FINISH
Microwave on medium for 4 minutes, or gently reheat in a saucepan.

Burrito

The most crucial thing to remember with this behemoth is that the meat is slow-cooked. This isn't much cop with a rare slice of sirloin, which will in all likelihood come out in a single piece, leaving you with a hollow, vegetarian burrito and a piece of pink flesh hanging out of your mouth. But slow-cooked beef shin, or brisket, or shortribs, or leftover pork shoulder, all melting and wibbly, will be what is known as 'the business'.

Prep time: 15 minutes

Cooking time: 6 minutes

Freezable? No

For the beans

150g/5½oz canned black-eyed beans

vegetable oil

1 small garlic clove, peeled and crushed

½ tsp smoked paprika

salt and pepper

juice of ½ lime

For the guacamole

1 avocado

2 tbsp finely chopped red onion

2 tsp finely chopped red chilli

juice of ½ lime

a small handful of chopped coriander (cilantro)

For the rest

2 large wheat tortillas

200g/7oz slow-cooked beef or pork

a good handful of shredded lettuce

chilli sauce (I like Cholula brand)

2 tbsp sour cream

AT HOME

Gently boil the beans for 5 minutes, then drain. In the same pan, heat a little oil over a medium heat and add the garlic and paprika. Cook for 30 seconds, stirring continuously, then add the beans. Season with salt, pepper and a squeeze of lime, then mash roughly. Set aside to cool.

To make the guacamole, mash the avocado with the onion, chilli, lime juice and coriander. Season with salt.

Briefly warm each tortilla in a hot frying pan (this makes it easier to wrap), then lay on a sheet of foil. Spread the guacamole over the tortilla, then spread over the mashed beans. Lay the meat down the middle of the tortilla, and top with lettuce, a few sploshes of chilli sauce, and a spoonful of sour cream. Carefully roll up, then wrap tightly in the foil.

IN EACH LUNCHBOX

A burrito.

TO FINISH

You can eat the burrito cold — or at least at room temperature — though it's also good hot. Warm in the oven at 150°C/300°F/Gas mark 2 for 10 minutes. The foil causes problems with microwaves... ka-boom.

SPICED LAMB BUNS

These are quite nifty for a picnic or a long walk, particularly if made smaller, though as a big bun with a surprise filling they're deeply moreish. The recipe makes more than two people will manage at lunch, but the buns freeze very well, or alternatively will make you very popular in your office.

Prep time: 30 minutes, plus rising time
Cooking time: 40 minutes
Freezable? Yes

500g/1lb 2oz/4 cups strong white bread flour, plus extra for dusting
7g/¼oz/about 1 tsp fast-action dried yeast
250ml/9fl oz/1 cup warm water
4 tbsp olive oil
3 tbsp plain yogurt
1 tsp salt

For the filling

1 onion, peeled and finely chopped
olive oil
1 garlic clove, peeled and finely chopped
1 tsp ground cumin
2 tsp ground coriander
1 tsp chilli flakes
salt and pepper
400g/14oz leftover lamb, chicken or beef, chopped

AT HOME

Tip the flour into a bowl and make a well in the centre. Pour in the yeast, water, oil, yogurt and salt. Mix the wet ingredients together then, using your hand like a claw, bring in the flour, adding a little warm water or olive oil if necessary. When it has all come together, turn it onto a lightly floured surface.

Knead for about 7 minutes, until smooth and elastic. Cover with a tea towel and leave to rise in a warm place for 30 minutes.

To make the filling, cook the onion in a little oil until golden and soft, then add the garlic and spices and season with salt and pepper. Stir for a minute or so, then mix through the chopped meat.

Divide the dough into 4 large or 8 small balls. Roll out each ball on a lightly floured surface to a round about 8mm/³/₈in thick. Put a good handful of the filling in the centre. Fold the outsides into the middle and pinch to seal. Place, seam-side down, on a lightly floured baking sheet. Repeat for the remaining dough, then cover with a tea towel and leave to rise in a warm place for another 30 minutes.

Preheat the oven to 220°C/425°F/Gas mark 7. Brush the tops of the buns with a little olive oil, then put in the oven. Turn the heat down to 190°C/375°F/Gas mark 5 and bake for 25–30 minutes. Cool on a wire rack.

IN EACH LUNCHBOX

A lamb bun or two.

TO FINISH

Serve cold, or reheat in a microwave on medium for 3 minutes, or in an oven at 150°C/300°F/Gas mark 2 for 10 minutes.

CHAPTER 2
SUPER NOODLES

A big bowl of slippery noodles is one of the finest and most comforting lunches there is, and we've seen some great strides in this country since the not-long-ago days of sachets and ominously flavoured concoctions (bacon noodles?). All the companies making these largely tasteless, synthetic and sachet-enhanced noodles are onto one thing, however, even if they don't necessarily get it right. You can inject a lot of flavour into a simple noodle and broth dish with a relatively small amount of cajolement.

Most of the recipes in this chapter come with a 'ShotPot', a little pot of concentrated flavours that you can bring to work safely, instead of having a precarious Tupperware-full of soup sloshing around on the bus. Then all you need to do is boil a kettle and pour the water over your noodles along with the ShotPot.

These recipes were tested with dried noodles, but fresh are nice, should you prefer (double the weight of noodles if using fresh).

EGG NOODLES WITH TOFU, CHILLI AND LEMONGRASS

I find it rather a shame that tofu is so maligned, so misinterpreted as the pinko-vegetarian's meat substitute of choice. I and many other enthusiastic carnivores enjoy tofu for its mellow silkiness, for its unobtrusive yet very present personality, and for its pure versatility.

This is a relatively cool dish, temperature-wise, though somewhat more fiery in spice.

Prep time: 10 minutes

Cooking time: 30 minutes

Freezable? No

For the ShotPot

400ml/14fl oz/1²/₃ cups chicken stock

1 shallot, peeled and roughly chopped

1 garlic clove, squashed with the flat of a knife

¹/₂ stalk of lemongrass, finely chopped

1 red chilli, sliced

2 tbsp soy sauce

For the rest

2-4 nests (100-150g/3¹/₂-5¹/₂oz) of egg noodles

150g/5¹/₂oz silken tofu, cubed (available in most supermarkets)

1 red chilli, deseeded and finely sliced

2 spring onions (scallions), thinly sliced

a few coriander (cilantro) leaves

AT HOME

Put all the ShotPot ingredients in a saucepan and bring to a gentle simmer. Simmer over a medium-low heat until reduced to 150-200ml/5-7fl oz/about ³/₄ cup. Leave to cool, strain through a sieve, then store in two jars in the fridge for up to 5 days.

Cook the noodles as per packet instructions, then run under cold water until cool. Divide between two heatproof containers along with the tofu, chilli and spring onions, and store in the fridge for up to 2 days.

IN EACH LUNCHBOX

A portion of noodles with tofu, chilli and spring onions (in a heatproof vessel); a ShotPot; fresh coriander leaves.

TO FINISH

Mix about 100ml/3¹/₂fl oz/scant ¹/₂ cup boiling water with the ShotPot, then pour this over the noodles. Stir and leave to stand for 1 minute. Garnish with coriander and serve.

Vietnamese beef noodle soup

My wife Rosie and I spent our honeymoon in Vietnam, an extraordinary country with some of the best food I've had anywhere. That said, it was with a degree of caution that we approached one particular lunch, at a tiny stall on a crowded backstreet in Hanoi, around which flies buzzed and on whose neighbouring stalls the viscera of countless animals hummed in the heat. It turned out to be the finest bowl of *pho*, Vietnamese noodle soup, that we had all holiday. This is my stab at that ubiquitous dish.

Prep time: 15–20 minutes

Cooking time: 30 minutes

Freezable? No

For the ShotPot

400ml/14fl oz/1²/₃ cups chicken or beef stock

2 tbsp Thai fish sauce

1 star anise

1 clove

1/2 tsp ground cinnamon

a few slices of fresh ginger

1 garlic clove, squashed with the flat of a knife

1 shallot, peeled and sliced

1 red chilli, deseeded and sliced

2 tsp sugar

For the rest

2 bundles (100–150g/3¹/₂–5¹/₂oz) of
    rice vermicelli noodles

200g/7oz beef rump steak

salt and pepper

vegetable oil

a handful of bean sprouts

a good handful of coriander (cilantro) leaves

lime wedges

a few Thai basil leaves (optional)

1 bird's-eye chilli, finely sliced (optional)

AT HOME

Put all the ShotPot ingredients in a saucepan and bring to a boil. Simmer over a medium–low heat until reduced to 150–200ml/5–7fl oz/about ³/₄ cup. Leave to cool. Discard the bits, and store in two jars in the fridge for up to 5 days.

Cook the noodles as per packet instructions, then run under cold water until cool. Set aside.

Season the steak on both sides, and rub with oil. Heat a heavy pan, add the steak, and cook for 2–3 minutes on each side. Set aside until cool.

Slice the meat (adding any juices to the ShotPot) and divide between two heatproof containers with the noodles and bean sprouts. Cover and store in the fridge for up to 2 days.

IN EACH LUNCHBOX

A portion of noodles, steak and bean sprouts (in a heatproof vessel); a ShotPot; fresh coriander; lime wedges; Thai basil and sliced chilli (optional).

TO FINISH

Tip the ShotPot over the noodles, then pour over 400–500ml/about 16fl oz/2 cups boiling water. Stir, then leave to stand for 1 minute. Garnish with coriander, lime, and Thai basil and chilli if using.

THAI CHICKEN NOODLE SOUP

There's something about Thai food – the nostril–clearing, punchy flavours combined with rich, coconutty broths and curries – that makes it irresistible. I find thigh meat far preferable, in this soup, to breast, but if you want to speed things up a bit, then just poach sliced chicken breast for 5 minutes. You could also use leftover roast chicken.

Prep time: 15 minutes

Cooking time: 1 hour

Freezable? No

For the ShotPot

vegetable oil

1 shallot, peeled and finely chopped

1 garlic clove, peeled and crushed

1 bird's–eye chilli, finely sliced

1/2 stalk of lemongrass, finely chopped

2 tsp grated fresh ginger

2 tbsp finely chopped coriander (cilantro) stalks

400ml/14fl oz/1 2/3 cups chicken stock

150ml/5fl oz/2/3 cup coconut cream

1 tbsp Thai fish sauce

zest of 1 lime

2 boneless chicken thighs

For the rest

100g/31/2oz flat rice noodles

50g/13/4oz mangetout (snow peas), roughly torn

a good handful of coriander (cilantro) leaves

2 lime wedges

AT HOME

Heat a little oil in a saucepan over a medium heat and cook the shallot, garlic, chilli, lemongrass, ginger and coriander stalks for 1 minute, stirring. Add the stock, coconut cream, fish sauce and lime zest, and bring to a gentle boil. Now add the chicken and simmer quietly for 30 minutes.

Remove the chicken. Continue to simmer the stock until reduced to about 200ml/7fl oz/generous 3/4 cup. Divide between two jars, cool and store in the fridge for up to 2 days.

Shred the cooled chicken. Cook the noodles according to packet instructions, then run under cold water until cool. Divide between two heatproof vessels, along with the mangetout and shredded chicken. Cover and chill for up to 2 days.

IN EACH LUNCHBOX

A portion of noodles, mangetout and chicken (in a heatproof vessel); a ShotPot; fresh coriander and a lime wedge.

TO FINISH

Tip the ShotPot over the noodles, then pour over 300ml/10fl oz/11/4 cups boiling water. Stir and leave to stand for 1 minute. Garnish with coriander and a squeeze of lime.

PRAWN NOODLE SALAD

Pad Thai, that backpackers' favourite, is the inspiration here, though this version is served cold. No ShotPot this time – just lots of crunch and spice and herbs and citrus.

Prep time: 15 minutes

Cooking time: 5 minutes

Freezable? No

100g/3½oz flat rice noodles

150g/5½oz cooked prawns (shrimp)

1 carrot, peeled and sliced into matchsticks

a good handful of bean sprouts

a good handful of sugar snap peas

a handful of peanuts, roughly chopped

a handful of coriander (cilantro) leaves

For the dressing

1 shallot, peeled and finely sliced

1 red chilli, deseeded and finely sliced

1 tbsp Thai fish sauce

juice of ½ lime

1 tbsp groundnut (peanut) oil

1 tsp palm or caster (superfine) sugar

AT HOME

Cook the noodles as per packet instructions, then run under cold water until cool. Divide between two Tupperwares or other lunchtime vessels along with the prawns, carrot, bean sprouts, sugar snaps, peanuts and coriander. Store in the fridge for up to 2 days.

To make the dressing, put all the ingredients in a bowl and whisk together. Store in a jar for up to 2 days.

IN EACH LUNCHBOX

A portion of salad; a portion of dressing.

TO FINISH

Dress, stir, devour.

Hanoi Kitchen's Bun Bo

This recipe comes courtesy of my friend Nigel, who runs a cracking street food stall called
Hanoi Kitchen. It's one of my favourite things in the world to eat. Hopefully my version comes close
to the perfection of Nigel's. Don't be put off by the long list of ingredients. This is very straightforward.

Prep time: 25 minutes
Cooking time: 30 minutes
Freezable? No

For the ShotPot
400ml/14fl oz/1 ²/₃ cups beef stock
1 tsp salt
2 tsp caster (superfine) sugar
2 tbsp rice vinegar
2 tbsp Thai fish sauce
juice of 1 lime
1 garlic clove, peeled and thinly sliced
¹/₂–1 Thai/bird's-eye chilli, finely sliced
¹/₂ stalk of lemongrass, finely chopped

For the pickled carrot
1 carrot, peeled into strips
200ml/7fl oz/generous ³/₄ cup water
3 tbsp rice vinegar
2 tbsp sugar
1 tsp salt

For the rest
200g/7oz rump steak, trimmed of excess fat
vegetable oil
100–150g/3¹/₂– 5¹/₂ oz rice vermicelli noodles
1 little gem lettuce, sliced
a handful of bean sprouts
a handful of coriander (cilantro) leaves
a handful of Thai basil leaves (or mint)
1 shallot, finely sliced
2 tbsp crushed roasted peanuts

AT HOME
Put all the ShotPot ingredients in a saucepan and
bring to a boil, stirring to dissolve the sugar. Simmer
over a medium–low heat for about 20 minutes,
until reduced to 150–200ml/5–7fl oz/about ³/₄ cup.
Cool. Store in two jars in the fridge for up to 5 days.

To pickle the carrot: mix the water, vinegar, sugar
and salt until all is dissolved, then pour over the
carrot strips. Set aside for at least 20 minutes.

Season the steak with salt and pepper, and rub
with oil. Heat a heavy pan and cook the steak for
2–3 minutes on each side. Rest on a plate until cold,
then slice. Add any juices to the ShotPot.

Cook the noodles as per packet instructions,
then run under cold water until cool. Take the carrots
out of their pickling juice and put in heatproof
containers with the noodles, lettuce and beef. Store
in the fridge for up to 2 days.

IN EACH LUNCHBOX
A portion of noodles, beef and lettuce (in a
heatproof vessel); a ShotPot; bean sprouts,
coriander, Thai basil, shallot and peanuts.

TO FINISH
Add the ShotPot to the noodles, then pour over
about 250ml/9fl oz/1 cup boiling water. Stir and
leave to stand for 1 minute. Finish with the bean
sprouts, coriander, basil, shallot and peanuts.

CHICKEN NOODLE SALAD

This is based on a bang bang salad, so called because you beat the hell out of the chicken before cooking it, and then add enough chilli that the stuff explodes in your mouth. But that's entirely up to you.

Prep time: 20 minutes
Cooking time: 40 minutes
Freezable? No

For the ShotPot
1 tsp sunflower or groundnut (peanut) oil
1 shallot, peeled and roughly chopped
1 garlic clove, peeled and roughly chopped
1 Thai chilli, finely sliced
2 chicken breasts
1 tbsp rice vinegar
juice of 1/2 lime
1 tsp salt
500ml/18fl oz/2 cups chicken stock
2 tbsp peanut butter

For the rest
2 bundles (100–150g/3½– 5½ oz) of
    rice vermicelli noodles
1 little gem lettuce, sliced
1 carrot, peeled and cut into matchsticks
a good handful of bean sprouts
a good handful of coriander (cilantro)
a few cashew nuts
lime wedges

AT HOME

Heat the oil in a saucepan over a low heat, add the shallot, garlic and chilli, and cook gently. Meanwhile, halve the chicken breasts horizontally and put the pieces between sheets of clingfilm. Beat with a rolling pin or your fists until flattened.

Add the vinegar, lime juice, salt and stock to the pan and bring to a boil. Lower in the chicken and poach over a medium–low heat for 8–10 minutes. Remove the chicken and leave to cool. Simmer the cooking liquor for another 15 minutes, until reduced to 150–200ml/5–7fl oz/about 3/4 cup. Stir in the peanut butter and leave to cool. Store in two jars in the fridge for up to 5 days.

Cook the noodles as per packet instructions, then run under cold water until cool. Put in your lunchboxes with the lettuce, carrot and bean sprouts. Shred the cooled chicken and chuck this in too. Cover and store in the fridge for up to 2 days.

IN EACH LUNCHBOX

A portion of noodles, chicken and vegetables; a ShotPot; fresh coriander, cashew nuts, lime wedges.

TO FINISH

Tip the ShotPot over the noodle salad and give it a good stir. Garnish with coriander, cashew nuts and lime wedges.

CHAPTER 3
THINGS ON TOAST

This chapter, it probably goes without saying, requires a toaster being to hand at lunchtime. Based on a straw poll, most people seem to have one in their office, so we should be OK here. If you don't, then this might be the time to petition for one – a toaster at work is a sure way to improve team morale. Toast is the great comforter of mankind. If there's butter, all the better.

As for bread – something of a revolution has happened in the past few years, with sales of bog–standard sliced bread falling and sales of 'proper' loaves, if not quite going through the roof, certainly gaining traction. For my part, I would say buy what you can afford. Good bread is worth the extra couple of quid, on the whole, but in some instances your average slice of wholemeal does the job quite merrily. Toast is a treat, whatever it's made from.

Purple sprouting broccoli, poached egg, anchovy dressing

You may be wondering how to go about poaching an egg in the office kitchen at lunchtime, but the trick is to poach it in your own kitchen at home, and reheat later. The delicate part comes in getting the egg from A to B without breaking what should be a perfectly poached egg, but with a bit of care and a not-too-rambunctious commute it shouldn't be too difficult.

Prep time: 15 minutes
Cooking time: 5 minutes
Freezable? No

2 fresh eggs
salt and pepper
200g/7oz purple sprouting broccoli
4 anchovy fillets
1 tbsp crème fraîche
1 tsp Dijon mustard
2 tsp white wine vinegar
4 tsp olive oil
bread for toasting
butter (optional)
a little grated Parmesan cheese (optional)

AT HOME

Bring a pan of water to just under a boil. Carefully break in the eggs (it helps to break them into a different vessel first, like an espresso cup) and gently poach for 3 minutes. Remove with a slotted spoon and transfer to a bowl of iced water. Leave to cool completely, then store in a covered container in the fridge for up to 2 days.

Bring a fresh pan of water to a boil with a pinch of salt. Simmer the broccoli for 1 minute, drain, then run under cold water until cool. Store in the fridge for up to 2 days.

To make the dressing, finely chop the anchovy fillets and mix with the crème fraîche and mustard. Stir in the vinegar and oil, season with pepper, and store in a small jar or two.

IN EACH LUNCHBOX

A poached egg; a portion of blanched broccoli; dressing; bread for toasting; butter and Parmesan (optional).

TO FINISH

Put the toast on. Boil a kettle and fill a mug or bowl with boiling water. Lower in the poached egg and leave for 1 minute. Butter the toast, if you want, and top with the broccoli and the poached egg. Finish with dressing and a little Parmesan if you like.

LABNEH, RADISH, LEMON AND OLIVE OIL

Anyone who owns any of my other books (and they are available in fine bookshops everywhere) may know of my fondness for curds, or, as they are known in the eastern Mediterranean, *labneh*. This is simply good yogurt (cow's, sheep's or goat's) strained for a day or two to get rid of the whey, leaving you with a rich, mild-flavoured cream cheese-esque number. It's a handy thing to have in the fridge as a pepper-upper of a soup or salad, or as the leading role in something like this.

Prep time: 5 minutes, plus 24 hours straining
Freezable? No

500g/1lb 2oz/2 cups plain yogurt
salt and pepper
2 tbsp olive oil
juice of ¹/₂ lemon
bread for toasting
1 garlic clove, halved (optional)
a handful of radishes

AT HOME

Line a bowl with a clean tea towel or muslin, and tip in the yogurt. Add a pinch of salt and give it a stir. Tie the corners of the tea towel together to make a bag, then hang from a cupboard handle, with the bowl underneath to catch the whey. Leave for 24–48 hours. Store in the fridge for up to a week.

Mix the olive oil and lemon juice, season with salt and pepper, and store in a jar.

IN EACH LUNCHBOX

A portion of curd; lemon dressing; bread for toasting; ¹/₂ garlic clove (optional); radishes.

TO FINISH

Toast the bread and rub with a little garlic, if using. Generously spread with the curd. Cut up a few radishes and scatter on top. Finish with the dressing and a twist of pepper.

CELERIAC REMOULADE WITH SMOKED SALMON AND WALNUTS

Odds are that after making this classic French number, you'll have some celeriac left kicking around. No bad thing. It'll keep for a good while wrapped in clingfilm in the fridge, and can be used for all sorts – soup, roasted with other veg (p.10), or sliced and baked with cream.

Prep time: 10 minutes

Freezable? No

125g/4¹/₂oz celeriac, peeled and grated

4 tbsp mayonnaise

2 tsp grainy mustard

a good squeeze of lemon juice

a small handful of parsley, finely chopped

salt and pepper

100g/3¹/₂oz smoked salmon

a small handful of walnuts, roughly chopped

bread for toasting

AT HOME

Mix the celeriac with the mayonnaise, mustard, lemon juice and parsley. Season with salt and pepper, cover and chill.

IN EACH LUNCHBOX

A portion of remoulade; 50g/1³/₄oz smoked salmon; chopped walnuts; bread for toasting.

TO FINISH

Make some toast and top it generously with the remoulade, smoked salmon, and a few chopped walnuts.

Avocado with burnt spring onion, chilli and lime sour cream

This sour cream dressing is pretty mega, and I'd recommend you employ it in as many permutations as you can – on steaks, barbecued chicken, grilled fish, that sort of thing. It's inspired by a recipe in Anthony Myint's excellent *Mission Street Food*. He recommends burning the spring onion until it's 'as black as your soul', though in all honesty I tend to wimp out somewhere short of that.

Prep time: 15 minutes
Cooking time: 5 minutes
Freezable? No

8 spring onions (scallions), trimmed
2 tsp finely chopped red chilli
1/2 garlic clove, peeled and crushed to a paste
juice of 1/2 lime
6 tbsp sour cream
salt and pepper
2 ripe avocados
bread for toasting – sourdough or granary
olive oil

AT HOME
Get a griddle or heavy frying pan really hot.
Add the spring onions and leave to char, turning occasionally, for about 5 minutes. Take off the heat and finely chop.
  Mix the chopped onion with the chilli, garlic, lime juice and sour cream. Season with salt and pepper, cover and store in the fridge for up to 5 days.

IN EACH LUNCHBOX
An avocado; a portion of spring onion sour cream; bread for toasting; olive oil.

TO FINISH
Toast some bread. Drizzle with olive oil. Halve an avocado, remove the stone, scoop out the good bits with a spoon and top the toast with them. Spoon over the sour cream dressing and eat.

Chorizo and mushroom ragout with a poached egg

Of all the fridge-lurkers and store-cupboard staples, I always find chorizo one of the most welcome. It has a nifty ability to perk up the most ascetic of suppers with its sweet, spicy smokiness. I'm a particular fan of the raw, 'cooking' chorizo, if you can get hold of it.

Prep time: 20 minutes
Cooking time: 25 minutes
Freezable? The ragout is, yes

olive oil
100g/3¹/₂oz chorizo sausage, roughly chopped
1 red onion, peeled and roughly chopped
1 garlic clove, peeled and thinly sliced
1 celery stalk, chopped
salt and pepper
150g/5¹/₂oz button or chestnut (cremini)
    mushrooms, halved
3 tbsp red wine
100g/3¹/₂oz chopped tomatoes (canned or fresh)
1 tbsp tomato purée (tomato paste)
2 eggs
bread for toasting – sourdough or granary
a handful of parsley, roughly chopped

AT HOME

Heat a little oil in a saucepan over a medium heat and add the chorizo. Fry until crisp and the oil in the pan is russet, then remove with a slotted spoon.

Add the onion, garlic and celery, season with salt and pepper, and cover. Cook for 10 minutes until soft, stirring occasionally.

Return the chorizo to the pan along with the mushrooms and wine. Simmer over a high heat for a minute, then add the tomatoes and tomato purée. Cover and cook for 10 minutes over a low heat. Cool, then store in the fridge for up to 3 days.

Bring a small pan of water to just under a boil and gently poach the eggs for 3 minutes. Remove with a slotted spoon and transfer to a bowl of cold water. When cool, store in a pot in the fridge.

IN EACH LUNCHBOX

A portion of ragout; a poached egg; bread for toasting; chopped parsley.

TO FINISH

Reheat the ragout in a microwave on medium for 3–4 minutes, or in a saucepan over a low heat. Put some toast on. Boil the kettle and pour into a mug or bowl. Lower in the poached egg and leave for 1 minute. Spoon the ragout over the toast, top with the poached egg, and garnish with chopped parsley.

Cucumber, feta and chilli

Cucumber might seem like an odd thing to bung on toast, but this tastes divine, if I say so myself. Generosity with the lemon and the oil will do you well.

Prep time: 10 minutes

Freezable? No

1/2 cucumber

2 tsp finely chopped red chilli

6 mint leaves, roughly torn

juice of 1/2 lemon

3 tbsp olive oil

salt and pepper

100g/3 1/2oz feta, crumbled

bread for toasting

AT HOME

Peel the cucumber then slice in half down the middle. Using a teaspoon, scoop out the seeds and discard. Chop the cucumber into 2cm/3/4in dice and mix with the chilli, mint, lemon juice and olive oil. Season with salt and pepper, cover and chill.

IN EACH LUNCHBOX

A portion of cucumber and feta salad; bread for toasting.

TO FINISH

Toast the bread. Top with the cucumber doings, then crumble over the feta. Finish with a pinch of salt.

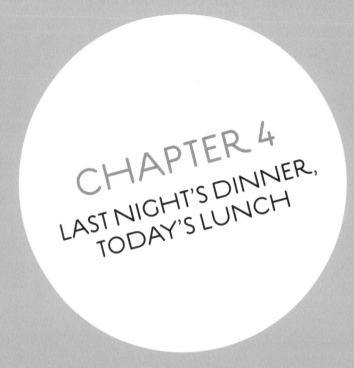

CHAPTER 4
LAST NIGHT'S DINNER, TODAY'S LUNCH

I have absolutely no idea what you eat for dinner most nights. Perhaps you roast a goose and make your own yogurt. Maybe you have a bowl of cereal. Nonetheless, I've hazarded a guess at what you might consider eating for dinner, and which you could very easily augment – a bit of chicken, some aubergine, rice, spuds... These are things that are easy to double up on when cooking: if you're boiling some potatoes, you might as well chuck in a few more for tomorrow's lunch; if you're firing up the oven to bake an aubergine, why not bake a couple more? That sort of thing.

None of the recipes preclude you making them specially if you so fancy.

CHILLED POTATO SOUP WITH WATERCRESS PESTO

Don't be tempted to try and whiz up cold potatoes (you will end up with something approaching glue) – but heating them through in stock will give you a silky vichyssoise, near-as-dammit.

Prep time: 15 minutes
Cooking time: 20 minutes
Freezable? No

25g/1oz/2 tbsp butter
1 onion, peeled and chopped
1 leek, chopped
salt and pepper
200g/7oz cooked new potatoes, roughly chopped
500ml/18fl oz/2 cups chicken stock
100ml/3^1/$_2$fl oz/scant ^{1}/$_2$ cup single (light) cream
For the pesto
25g/1oz watercress
2 tbsp walnuts
1 small garlic clove, peeled
2 tbsp grated Parmesan cheese
4 tbsp olive oil

AT HOME

Melt the butter in a saucepan over a lowish heat and add the onion and leek. Season with salt and pepper, cover and cook for 15 minutes, stirring occasionally, until soft.

Add the potatoes and stock and bring to a boil. Simmer for 8–10 minutes, then blend until smooth. Stir in the cream, cool, then chill in the fridge for up to 2 days.

For the pesto, put the watercress, walnuts, garlic and Parmesan in a blender or pestle and mortar, and blend/pound until smooth. Beat in the olive oil along with a pinch of salt and pepper, and store in a jar in the fridge.

IN EACH LUNCHBOX

A portion of chilled potato soup; a portion of watercress pesto.

TO FINISH

Put a dollop of pesto in your soup and eat.

New potato, smoked mackerel and boiled egg salad

Reluctant as I am to suggest using your lunch as a sort of graveyard for the fridge's odds and ends, you could in theory be somewhat more extravagant with the contents of this salad – some blanched green beans would work nicely, for example, or a handful of black olives – but I've kept this simple for now.

Don't cut up the egg until you're ready to eat or you'll lose all the lovely yolk.

Prep time: 10 minutes
Cooking time: 5 minutes
Freezable? No

2 fresh eggs
250g/9oz cooked new potatoes
2 fillets smoked mackerel, skinned and flaked
2 little gem lettuces, washed and roughly torn
a handful of parsley leaves

For the dressing
1 tbsp Dijon mustard or horseradish sauce
1 tbsp white wine vinegar
3 tbsp olive oil
a pinch of sugar
salt and pepper

AT HOME

First, make the dressing: shake all the ingredients together in a jar, along with a pinch of salt and pepper. Set aside.

Boil the eggs for 5 minutes, then transfer to a bowl of iced water. Leave until cool, then peel.

In two – safely transportable – containers, assemble the potatoes, smoked mackerel, lettuce and parsley. Carefully sit an egg among the leaves.

IN EACH LUNCHBOX

A portion of salad; a portion of dressing.

TO FINISH

Quarter the egg. Dress the salad. Eat.

POACHED CHICKEN

There are several good reasons to poach a chicken – it's healthier than roasting, the chances of you overcooking the thing to a dry, crumbly disappointment are fewer, and when you've finished, you're left with a ready–made stock. Here's how you do it:

Get a chicken, about 1.5kg/3lb 5oz. Ideally, let it come up to room temperature.

Get a big pan. One big enough for the bird with room besides. Put all or as many of the following as you can in: 1/2 onion, a celery stalk, a bulb of garlic halved through its equator, a carrot, a leek, 1 tsp salt, peppercorns, a clove, a handful of thyme, a bay leaf, a large glass (about 200ml/7fl oz/generous 3/4 cup) of white wine. Fill the pan about three–quarters full with water. Bring to a boil. Gently introduce the chicken. Reduce the heat to a gentle simmer. Poach for 1 1/2 hours.

Remove, rest for 15 minutes. Carve. Serve.

Now you have a pan of beautiful chicken stock and, with any luck, some leftover chicken. Here are two lunch recipes that use them:

Tortellini broth

Years ago my friend Ali worked in the legendary Vecchia Scuola pasta school in Bologna. To the horror of the Italians, he went on to win the junior 'Golden Rolling Pin' award. They didn't like that. A blond Briton, making better pasta than the Italians. He once made this for me. It's surprisingly heartening and richly flavoured.

I don't expect you to make your own pasta, but feel it would be a bit of a cop out for me not to include a recipe. By all means buy some tortellini from a shop. But should you find yourself with a spare hour on a Sunday, then it's fun to do. You'll need a microwave if you don't have a hob.

Prep time: 25 minutes, plus resting time
Cooking time: 5 minutes
Freezable? Yes

100g/3¹/₂oz/generous ³/₄ cup sifted plain (all-
    purpose) flour, or ideally Italian '00' pasta flour
1 large egg
50g/1³/₄oz leftover chicken
20g/³/₄oz parsley leaves
25g/1oz Parmesan cheese, plus extra to finish
2 tbsp olive oil
salt and pepper
500ml/18fl oz/2 cups chicken stock, to finish

AT HOME
To make the pasta: put the flour into a bowl and make a well in the middle. Weigh the contents of the egg. You're aiming for 65g: if it's less, add a little water; if it's more, add a little more flour. Drop the egg into the flour well and, using a fork, start to whisk the egg, gradually incorporating the flour from around the outside. When fully mixed, tip onto a work surface and knead. If absolutely necessary lightly flour the work surface, but try not to. After

7–10 minutes, the dough should feel like a stress ball. Wrap in clingfilm and chill for 30 minutes.

Meanwhile, put the chicken, parsley, Parmesan and olive oil in a blender with a pinch of salt and pepper and briefly whiz. Alternatively, chop well.

Cut the dough in half and then, using a pasta machine or a rolling pin, roll out the dough until you can read a newspaper through it. Trim the edges with a sharp knife, then cut into 4cm/1¹/₂in squares. Put a spoonful of chicken mixture in the centre of each square, brush the edges with a little water, and fold over to make a triangle. Press around the edges to seal, then fold the two corners of the longest side around your little finger and seal at the back. Cover and store in the fridge for up to a day, or freeze half.

IN EACH LUNCHBOX
250ml/9fl oz/1 cup stock (in a microwaveable vessel); a portion of tortellini; grated Parmesan.

TO FINISH
Warm the stock in a microwave on medium for 3 minutes. Add the tortellini and microwave for another 2 minutes. Sprinkle over a little Parmesan if you like and serve.

JAMBALAYA

Anyone who's seen the movie *Mrs Doubtfire* will be at least vaguely familiar with this dish, and may also know that ordering jambalaya without pepper is a bit like ordering chips without salt. Being a Southern dish, the wumph of pepper is fairly crucial. I don't think Robin Williams was so much trying to kill Pierce Brosnan as just cheer up his dinner. Anyway...

Jambalaya is traditionally made with a Franco–Louisianian smoked sausage called andouille, but you're more likely to find chorizo. If you can find andouille, then all the better.

Prep time: 20 minutes
Cooking time: 45 minutes
Freezable? Yes

sunflower or vegetable oil
50g/1¾oz chorizo, cubed
1 small red onion, peeled and chopped
1 garlic clove, peeled and sliced
1 celery stalk, chopped
½ red pepper, finely chopped
salt and pepper
1 tsp cayenne pepper
100g/3½oz leftover chicken, shredded
125g/4½oz/scant ¾ cup brown rice
300ml/10fl oz/1¼ cups chicken stock

AT HOME

Heat a little oil in a heavy–bottomed saucepan and fry the chorizo until crisp. Add the onion, garlic, celery and red pepper, and season with salt and pepper. Cover and cook over a low heat for 15 minutes, until soft.

Stir in the cayenne and cook for a further minute, then add the chicken, rice and stock. Bring to a boil, cover, and simmer very gently for 30 minutes.

Keeping the lid on, remove from the heat and leave to stand for 5 minutes. Uncover and leave to cool. Store in the fridge for up to 2 days.

IN EACH LUNCHBOX

A portion of jambalaya (in a microwaveable vessel).

TO FINISH

Eat cold, or microwave on medium for 4–5 minutes, stirring halfway through.

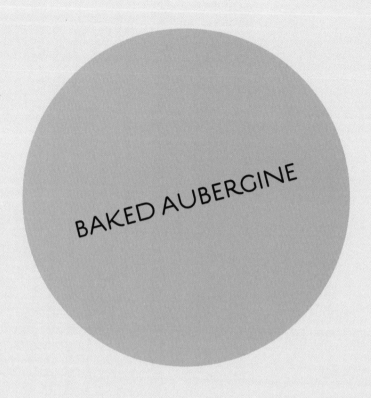

BAKED AUBERGINE

Not quite a dinner in itself, but a simple and frugal foundation for all sorts of loveliness. Halved down the middle and slashed a few times, the aubergine becomes a sponge for other flavours – a splosh of olive oil and a few slices of garlic, or a more involved blend of spices mixed with honey and oil and herbs – then just needs baking at 200°C/400°F/Gas mark 6 for 30–40 minutes. Serve with whatever's appropriate – a dollop of yogurt, warm flatbreads and tabbouleh; rice, soy sauce and greens; crumbled feta and chilli...

And if you're going to fire up the oven, you might as well make the most of the energy and cook extra for tomorrow's lunch. Here are a couple of things to do with bonus 'bergines:

AUBERGINE SALAD WITH BULGUR WHEAT AND HALLOUMI

There's a Middle Eastern vibe to this salad. If you can't get hold of preserved lemons, or don't like them, use the grated zest of a lemon instead.

Prep time: 20 minutes
Cooking time: 25 minutes
Freezable? No

2 tbsp olive oil
125g/4½oz halloumi cheese, sliced
1 onion, peeled and sliced
1 garlic clove, peeled and finely chopped
1 tsp *ras-el-hanout* (spice blend available in most supermarkets)
100g/3½oz bulgur wheat
1 aubergine (eggplant), baked as left, sliced
1 preserved lemon, flesh discarded, peel finely chopped
a good handful of parsley, finely chopped
salt and pepper

AT HOME

Heat 1 tbsp of the oil in a large frying pan over a medium-high heat and add the halloumi. Fry on both sides until browned and crisp, then drain on kitchen paper.

Heat the remaining oil in a saucepan and gently cook the onion and garlic, stirring regularly, until soft. Stir in the *ras-el-hanout* and cook for a further minute, stirring all the while. Now fold through the bulgur wheat and add 200ml/7fl oz/ generous ¾ cup water. Bring to a gentle boil, cover, and simmer for 15 minutes. Keeping the lid on, remove from the heat and leave to stand for 5 minutes.

Combine with the halloumi, aubergine, lemon and parsley, and season well with salt and pepper. Store in the fridge for up to 3 days.

IN EACH LUNCHBOX

A portion of aubergine and bulgur wheat salad.

TO FINISH

Eat.

SICHUAN SPICED AUBERGINE

This is based on the Sichuan favourite, fish fragrant aubergine. It's called 'fish fragrant' because it uses flavour combinations usually found in Sichuan fish dishes. The joke with this dish is that there's no fish anywhere near it. The aubergine is deep-fried, though, which in this recipe it isn't.

I gladly yomp this on its own, though you may wish to bulk it up with some microwaved rice.

Prep time: 12–15 minutes
Cooking time: 10 minutes
Freezable? Yes

sunflower oil
4 spring onions (scallions), finely chopped
2 garlic cloves, peeled and finely chopped
1 tbsp grated fresh ginger
2 red chillies, deseeded and finely chopped
2 aubergines (eggplants), baked as above, sliced
1 tsp sesame oil
2 tbsp soy sauce
2 tbsp tomato purée (tomato paste)
1 tbsp caster (superfine) sugar
salt and pepper
To garnish
sesame seeds
coriander (cilantro) leaves

AT HOME

Heat a little oil in a large pan over a medium-high heat. Add the spring onions, garlic, ginger and chillies, and stir-fry for a few minutes, until softened.

Add the aubergine, sesame oil, soy sauce, tomato purée and sugar. Season with a little salt and a twist of pepper, and stir in about 150ml/5fl oz/²/₃ cup water. Bring to a boil and simmer gently, uncovered, stirring occasionally, for 10 minutes, until thick, glossy and soft. Leave to cool, then cover and store in the fridge for up to 5 days.

IN EACH LUNCHBOX

A portion of aubergines (in a microwaveable vessel); sesame seeds and coriander.

TO FINISH

Reheat in a microwave on medium for 3–4 minutes. Serve garnished with coriander and sesame seeds.

RICE

I invariably cook too much rice. Sometimes this is greedy and intentional, though more often than not it's through carelessness and a lack of conviction – I know from much rice–cooking experience that one tumbler of rice will serve two of us, but will add a little extra just in case the glass has miraculously shrunk since its last outing.

Also, I just love the stuff: I happily eat it for lunch with a few greens and a splash of soy sauce, or simmered with stock and a few spices and eaten with a dollop of yogurt.

To cook basmati rice:

Measure about 75g/2³/₄oz rice per person. Rinse this in a sieve under a running tap until the water runs relatively clear. This gets rid of excess starch, and you'll find that some brands need less rinsing than others.

Tip the rice into a saucepan, and add double its volume in liquid (so for 75g/2³/₄oz/generous ¹/₃ cup rice, you want 150ml/5fl oz/²/₃ cup water). Add a pinch of salt and bring to a boil. Cover, reduce the heat right down and leave for 12 minutes. *Do not uncover.*

After 12 minutes, remove from the heat but *still do not uncover*. Leave to stand for 5 minutes, then take off the lid. Leave for a further 2 minutes to steam off any excess liquid. Fluff up with a fork and serve.

Leftover rice should be cooled as quickly as possible (tip out onto a baking sheet), then covered and refrigerated.

RICE AND FETA—STUFFED PEPPERS

This is unashamedly retro and unoriginal, but also kind of delicious and straightforward.

Prep time: 10 minutes

Cooking time: 30 minutes

Freezable? No

2 red peppers

a few slices of garlic

4 sprigs of thyme

salt and pepper

olive oil

150g/5$\frac{1}{2}$oz/scant 1 cup cooked rice

100g/3$\frac{1}{2}$oz feta cheese, crumbled

$\frac{1}{2}$ red onion, very finely chopped

about 2 tbsp chopped parsley

about 1 tbsp shredded mint

zest of $\frac{1}{2}$ lemon

AT HOME

Preheat the oven to 220°C/425°F/Gas mark 7. Halve the peppers and deseed. Place cut-side up on a baking sheet and pop a couple of slivers of garlic and a sprig of thyme in the cavities. Season with salt and pepper, add a glug of olive oil, and roast for 30 minutes. Leave to cool completely. Meanwhile, mix the rice, feta, red onion, parsley, mint and lemon zest, and add a little splash of olive oil. Season with salt and pepper and set aside. Stuff the rice mixture into the cooled roasted pepper halves. Store in the fridge for up to 2 days.

IN EACH LUNCHBOX

2 stuffed pepper halves (in a microwaveable vessel).

TO FINISH

Reheat in a microwave on medium for 4 minutes, or in an oven at 180°C/350°F/Gas mark 4 for 10 minutes.

TURKISH LAMB AND RICE BROTH

In the Turkish city of Antep, this soup – *beyran* – is traditionally eaten for breakfast, when it will cure even the most raging of raki–fuelled hangovers. In the most famous restaurant that serves it, one old boy has been there since, you would think, time began. He stands by a BBQ–type erection and will in a matter of seconds throw together your breakfast. A fistful of cooked rice goes into a metal serving dish along with slow–cooked mutton, a pinch of chilli flakes and a generous ladle of hot stock. It then sits over a ferocious flame until bubbling hot, before being frisbeed out to customers with a wedge of lemon and a large green chilli. You, the customer, eat it with fresh bread, and all is well in the world.

Prep time: 15 minutes

Cooking time: 1 hour 45 minutes

Freezable? No

250g/9oz lamb neck fillet (or 150g/5½oz shredded
    slow–cooked lamb)

salt and pepper

olive oil

1 small onion, finely chopped

2 garlic cloves, peeled and finely chopped

500ml/18fl oz/2 cups chicken stock

1 tomato, halved

1 bay leaf

about 100g/3½oz/⅔ cup cooked basmati or
    long–grain rice

dried chilli flakes

To serve

lemon wedges

a large green chilli (optional)

AT HOME

Season the lamb generously with salt and pepper. Heat a little oil in a saucepan over a high heat and brown the lamb for a couple of minutes on each side, until well coloured. Remove the lamb and reduce the heat.

Add the onion, and season with salt and pepper. Cover and cook for 7–10 minutes, until soft, then add the garlic, stock, tomato, bay leaf and lamb. Cover and simmer very gently for 1½ hours, until the lamb is very soft. Remove and leave the lamb to cool, then shred with a pair of forks. Reserve the stock.

When the lamb is completely cool, divide it between microwave–friendly dishes, along with the rice and a pinch of chilli flakes. Discard the tomato and the bay leaf from the stock and store the stock in a separate container in the fridge.

IN EACH LUNCHBOX

A portion of lamb and rice (in a microwaveable vessel); a portion of stock (about 300ml/10fl oz/ 1¼ cups); lemon wedge; green chilli (optional).

TO FINISH

Tip the stock over the rice and lamb, and microwave on medium for 4 minutes, stirring halfway through. Squeeze the lemon into the soup and garnish with the chilli, if using.

BAKED SWEET POTATO

I tend to feel guilty for sticking on the oven to bake potatoes when it's just two of us at home. All that energy for a baked potato seems a bit wrong. Sweet potatoes do take less time to cook than their non–sweet counterparts, but this is splitting hairs. So, when the urge for a baked sweet potato strikes, it's worth baking extra for lunch.

Bake sweet potatoes on a skewer in an oven preheated to 180°C/350°F/Gas mark 4 for 45 minutes to 1 hour, until tender.

Sweet potato, ginger and coconut soup

A lightly spiced soup for a cold, or indeed warm, day.

Prep time: 15 minutes

Cooking time: 15 minutes

Freezable? Yes

1 tbsp vegetable oil

1 red onion, peeled and chopped

1 garlic clove, peeled and chopped

salt and pepper

1 tbsp mild curry powder

1 tbsp grated fresh ginger

1 baked sweet potato

200ml/7fl oz/generous 3/4 cup coconut milk

400ml/14fl oz/1 2/3 cups chicken or
     vegetable stock

To serve

plain yogurt

coriander (cilantro) leaves

AT HOME

Heat the oil in a large pan and add the onion and garlic. Season with salt and pepper, and cook gently for 5–7 minutes, stirring regularly.

Add the curry powder and ginger and stir for 30 seconds, then scoop in the sweet potato (discarding the skin), the coconut milk and the stock. Bring to a boil, breaking up the potato with a spoon as you do, and simmer gently for 5 minutes, then blend until smooth. Cool, cover, and store in the fridge for up to 3 days.

IN EACH LUNCHBOX

A portion of soup (in a microwaveable container); yogurt and coriander.

TO FINISH

Reheat the soup on the hob or in a microwave on medium for 3–4 minutes. Serve with a dollop of yogurt and a few coriander leaves.

Sweet potato and chorizo quesadilla

Omit the chorizo if you prefer – meat-free Mondays and all that.

Prep time: 15 minutes

Cooking time: 10 minutes

Freezable? Yes

olive oil

50g/1¾oz chorizo, diced

½ red onion, finely chopped

1 baked sweet potato, skin discarded

50g/1¾oz Cheddar, grated

1 green chilli, deseeded and finely chopped

a squeeze of lime juice

a handful of coriander (cilantro), roughly chopped

a handful of spinach leaves

salt and pepper

2 soft corn tortillas

AT HOME

Heat a little oil in a frying pan, add the chorizo and fry until crisp. Add the onion and cook, stirring regularly, for a couple of minutes, until softened. Transfer to a bowl and beat in the potato flesh, cheese, chilli, lime, coriander and spinach. Season with salt and pepper to taste.

Spread this mixture over one of the tortillas and top with the other tortilla. Press down firmly, then fry for a couple of minutes on each side, until crisp (easiest way to turn is to flip it onto a plate and then slide it back into the pan). Leave on a wire rack to cool. Cut into quarters and store in the fridge for up to 2 days.

IN EACH LUNCHBOX

Half a quesadilla.

TO FINISH

Reheat the quesadilla, uncovered, in an oven at 180°C/350°F/Gas mark 4 for 5 minutes, or in a microwave on medium for 2 minutes. It's best reheated in the oven, but not disastrous in a microwave.

CHAPTER 5
COCKLE WARMERS

If ever there were a time to have a lovely hot lunch squirrelled away in the office, it's when sleet clobbers the windows and trees arch comically in the wind. This is not the time for trudging to the local chain to queue for a sandwich, but rather to stay indoors with a newspaper and a bowl of something nourishing. These recipes are written to comfort and warm, the food equivalent of a big fleece.

In such moments, a microwave is a useful asset. When I asked Twitter who had a microwave in their office, a straw poll returned a 100% result, but should you not, then now is the time to get one. Having never owned one myself – through lack of space as opposed to any kind of antipathy – I borrowed one for the purposes of this book, and am finding the prospect of returning it somewhat unappealing.

KALE AND BORLOTTI BEAN MINESTRONE

This is a somewhat slovenly dish, ideal for using up odds and ends from the fridge. If you can't find kale, or indeed borlotti, substitute savoy cabbage and butter beans or cannellini beans respectively.

Prep time: 15 minutes

Cooking time: 30 minutes

Freezable? Yes

2 tbsp olive oil

1 small onion, peeled and thinly sliced

1 garlic clove, peeled and thinly sliced

1 carrot, peeled and diced

1 celery stalk, finely chopped

a sprig of thyme

salt and pepper

100g/3½oz kale, roughly chopped

1 x 400g/14oz can borlotti beans, drained

400g/14oz canned chopped tomatoes

250ml/9fl oz/1 cup chicken stock

grated Parmesan cheese, to serve

AT HOME

Heat the oil in a saucepan over a low heat and add the onion, garlic, carrot, celery and thyme. Season with salt and pepper, cover and cook for 15–20 minutes, until good and soft.

Add the kale, beans, tomatoes and stock. Bring to a boil and simmer gently for 8 minutes. Taste for seasoning and add a pinch more salt if necessary. Leave to cool, then store in the fridge for up to 3 days.

IN EACH LUNCHBOX

A portion of minestrone (in a microwaveable vessel); Parmesan cheese.

TO FINISH

Reheat in a microwave on medium for 3–4 minutes. Scatter with Parmesan and eat.

Sausage and lentils

One of my all-time favourite partnerships, sausages and lentils go together like potatoes and cream, like bacon and eggs, like Posh and Becks. This is just what you need on a cold January lunchtime.

Prep time: 15 minutes

Cooking time: 1 hour

Freezable? Yes

olive oil

1 onion, peeled and thickly sliced

salt and pepper

4 decent, chunky sausages

125ml/4fl oz/½ cup red wine

1 bay leaf

mustard, to serve

For the lentils

1 small onion, peeled and finely chopped

1 garlic clove, peeled and finely chopped

100g/3½oz/½ cup green lentils

250ml/9fl oz/1 cup chicken stock

a good handful of parsley

AT HOME

Preheat the oven to 180°C/350°F/Gas mark 4. Heat a little oil in an ovenproof frying pan or saucepan and gently cook the onion until softened. Season with salt and pepper, then nestle in the sausages and cook until lightly browned. Add the wine and the bay leaf. Simmer for a couple more minutes, then bake in the oven for 45 minutes. If the wine reduces and the onions start to catch, so much the better, but take care not to let them burn. Add a drop of water if necessary.

Meanwhile, for the lentils, cook the onion and garlic in a little oil in a saucepan over a low heat until soft. Add the lentils and stock, and bring to a boil. Cover and simmer gently for 20–25 minutes until *al dente*. Season with salt and pepper, and stir through the parsley. Allow the lentils and sausages to cool, then cover and store in the fridge for up to 3 days.

IN EACH LUNCHBOX

A portion of sausage and lentils (in a microwaveable vessel).

TO FINISH

Microwave on medium for 4–5 minutes. Serve with mustard.

AUBERGINE TAGINE WITH BULGUR WHEAT PILAF

You could get a bit more involved with this pilaf, cooking a vast amount of onion down for a long time and adding all sorts of spices, fruits and herbs. The result is delicious and worth the effort, if the timing's right, but if it's 9pm on a Monday evening you're not going to be in the mood for that, so this is a pared-down version.

Cooking time: 25 minutes

Prep time: 40 minutes

Freezable? Yes

For the tagine

olive oil

1/2 onion, peeled and finely chopped

1 garlic clove, peeled and sliced

1 tsp *ras-el-hanout* (spice blend available in most supermarkets)

salt and pepper

1 aubergine (eggplant), cut into 2.5cm/1in dice

200g/7oz chopped tomatoes (canned are fine)

For the bulgur pilaf

1/2 onion, peeled and thinly sliced

1 tsp ground cumin

2 tsp ground coriander

1/2 tsp ground cinnamon

100g/31/2oz bulgur wheat

200ml/7fl oz/generous 3/4 cup chicken or vegetable stock

2 tbsp raisins

2 tbsp flaked almonds or 1 tbsp pine nuts (optional)

To serve

plain yogurt

a small handful of fresh coriander (cilantro)

AT HOME

For the tagine, heat a splash of oil in a saucepan and gently cook the onion and garlic until soft. Add the *ras-el-hanout* along with a good pinch of salt and a twist of pepper, and cook over a medium heat for 1 minute, stirring continuously. Add the aubergine and tomatoes, and about 150ml/5fl oz/2/3 cup water, stir to combine, then cover and cook for 15 minutes, until the aubergine is soft. Leave to cool. Cover and store in the fridge for up to 5 days.

For the pilaf, heat a splash of oil in a saucepan over a medium heat and cook the onion until soft and lightly browned. Stir in the spices and cook for a further minute, then add the bulgur wheat and stock. Bring to a boil, cover, and cook over the lowest heat for 15 minutes. Keeping the lid on, remove from the heat and leave to stand for 5 minutes. Stir through the raisins and almonds, if using. Cool, then cover and store in the fridge for up to 5 days.

IN EACH LUNCHBOX

A portion of aubergine tagine (in a microwaveable vessel); a portion of pilaf; yogurt and coriander.

TO FINISH

Microwave the aubergine on medium for 4 minutes, stirring halfway through. Serve with the pilaf.

Pea and coriander soup

This has been a favourite since my time at Darina Allen's Ballymaloe Cookery School, upon whose recipe this one is based.

Prep time: 15 minutes

Cooking time: 15 minutes

Freezable? Yes

2 tbsp olive oil

1 small onion, peeled and finely chopped

1 small garlic clove, peeled and sliced

1/2 green chilli, deseeded and finely chopped

salt and pepper

500ml/18fl oz/2 cups chicken or vegetable stock

300g/10½oz/2 cups frozen peas

15g/½oz coriander (cilantro) leaves

plain yogurt, to serve

AT HOME

Heat the oil in a saucepan over a lowish heat and add the onion, garlic and chilli. Season with salt and pepper, cover and cook for 10 minutes, until soft. Add the stock and bring to a boil. Add the peas and simmer for 3 minutes. Stir through the coriander leaves, then blend until smooth. Leave to cool, then store in the fridge for up to 3 days.

IN EACH LUNCHBOX

A portion of pea and coriander soup (in a microwaveable vessel); yogurt.

TO FINISH

Reheat the soup in a microwave on medium for 4 minutes, stirring halfway through. Give it a good stir and serve with a dollop of yogurt.

Mashed swede with meatballs

The poor swede is desperately under-appreciated, and I can't for the life of me work out why. Is it something to do with school food? Associations with rationing? Its deliciously pungent but undeniably unsexy aroma? Who knows? With butter and pepper, it's one of the greatest root vegetables you can pull from the earth.

Prep time: 25 minutes

Cooking time: 30 minutes

Freezable? Yes

For the meatballs

125g/4¹/₂oz fresh minced (ground) pork

125g/4¹/₂oz fresh minced (ground) beef

¹/₂ tsp chilli flakes

1 tsp fennel seeds, crushed

a small handful of parsley, finely chopped

salt and pepper

olive oil

1 small onion, peeled and very finely chopped

1 garlic clove, peeled and finely chopped

200g/7oz canned chopped tomatoes

For the mashed swede

1 small swede, peeled and cut into 2.5cm/1in dice

25–50g/1–1³/₄oz/2–4 tbsp butter

AT HOME

Mix the pork, beef, chilli, fennel and parsley, and season with salt and pepper. Form into about 10 meatballs. Heat a little oil in a sauté or frying pan and brown the meatballs all over. Remove to a plate.

Add the onions to the same pan, with another drop of oil if necessary. Season with salt and pepper, and cook gently until soft. Add the garlic and tomatoes, along with a splash of water, and bring to a gentle simmer. Return the meatballs to the pan and simmer for 10–12 minutes, until firm. Leave to cool.

Meanwhile, gently boil the swede in salted water until tender. Drain and shake off any excess liquid. Mash with the butter and plenty of pepper. Divide between two microwave-friendly containers and top with the meatballs. Cover and store in the fridge.

IN EACH LUNCHBOX

Portion of meatballs and mashed swede (in a microwaveable vessel).

TO FINISH

Reheat in a microwave on medium for 5 minutes.

CHAPTER 6
SUMMER LUNCHES

The writing of this book was concluded during that frighteningly hot month in July (to those with foreign editions, it does indeed happen occasionally in the UK), and having spent a few days testing recipes for the previous chapter, I must admit that coming to these was something of a relief. Even with all the kitchen windows open, it was still like cooking in a Cuban casino.

The chilled soups and vibrant salads were more welcome than you can imagine, and in turn gave me the opportunity to imagine you, in your office, face inches from a fan, in desperate need of something light and cooling. With any luck, these recipes will be just the thing, though they needn't be restricted to just the hottest days. Some are wholesome, virtuous dishes for any time of year.

A RAW SALAD OF ROOTS AND TOASTED NUTS

I once briefly – in the name of research – endured a raw vegan diet. A slightly barmy friend had assured me it would give me energy, clear skin, enormous brain power, and no beer belly. I can tell you, after two weeks all it gave me was a sense of despair and a very short temper. It did, however, leave me with a new appreciation of the beauty of raw roots, and particularly beetroot, in my view the star of the show here.

Prep time: 20 minutes

Cooking time: 2 minutes

Freezable? No

1 tsp cumin seeds, lightly crushed

1 tsp coriander seeds, lightly crushed

1 tbsp sesame seeds

1 tbsp pumpkin seeds

2–3 tbsp chopped hazelnuts

2–3 tbsp chopped pistachios

1 beetroot, peeled and grated

1 large carrot, peeled and grated

1 fennel bulb, finely sliced

a good handful (about 20g/¾oz) of parsley leaves

salt and pepper

For the dressing

juice of 1 lemon

3 tbsp olive oil

AT HOME

Put a dry frying pan over a medium–high heat and add the spices, seeds and nuts. Toast, shaking the pan occasionally, until fragrant. Take care not to burn but equally don't be too ginger – you want a bit of colour.

Put the beetroot, carrot and fennel in a bowl, scatter over the chopped parsley and toasted nuts and spices, and season with a little salt and pepper. Store in the fridge for up to 2 days.

For the dressing, shake together the lemon juice and olive oil in a jar, along with salt and pepper.

IN EACH LUNCHBOX

A portion of salad; a portion of dressing.

TO FINISH

Toss the dressing through the salad and eat.

Orzo with crispy cabbage and lemon and pine nuts

Amazing how easy it is to borrow a recipe without realizing it.

'I'm not entirely sure where this recipe came from', I began this introduction. 'Possibly just some strange and hungry backwater of my mind. Orzo is a kind of pasta that looks like fat grains of rice. If you can't find it, use macaroni instead...'.

After cooking it one evening, however, my wife Rosie pointed out that there is a recipe in her own book, *The Recipe Wheel*, that is nigh-on identical, save for the fact that she uses macaroni instead. So there you go. It's still here because, well, it's rather nice. But thanks to Ro for the idea.

Prep time: 5 minutes

Cooking time: 10 minutes

Freezable? No

200g/7oz orzo

salt and pepper

4 tbsp olive oil

1 garlic clove, peeled and thinly sliced

200g/7oz savoy cabbage, very finely sliced

zest and juice of $^1\!/_2$ lemon

1 tbsp pine nuts

grated Parmesan cheese, to serve

AT HOME

Bring a pan of salted water to a boil and cook the orzo according to packet instructions. Drain and run under a cold tap until cool.

Meanwhile, heat the oil in a large frying pan or saucepan over a medium-high heat, and briefly fry the garlic. Add the cabbage and season with salt and pepper. Cook for 5–7 minutes, stirring frequently, until the cabbage is cooked and crisp here and there. Stir in the lemon zest and juice and set aside.

In a dry frying pan, toast the pine nuts over a medium-high heat, taking care not to burn. Stir these and the cabbage through the pasta. Leave to cool and store in the fridge for up to 3 days.

IN EACH LUNCHBOX

A portion of orzo salad; grated Parmesan.

TO FINISH

Serve with a little grated Parmesan.

RED CAMARGUE RICE WITH MINT AND ALMONDS

This hardy, nutty rice is grown in the south of France and is a new favourite of mine. Come to that, it's pretty new to most people, having only been grown for 50 or so years. It's a little more expensive than your average rice, but worth the cheddar, in my opinion. Some recommend you cook it like risotto, but here the whole thing's a little more straightforward.

This recipe was inspired by one knocked out by Yotam Ottolenghi. What isn't, these days?

Prep time: 15 minutes

Cooking time: 35 minutes

Freezable? No

150g/5¹/₂oz/generous ³/₄ cup red Camargue rice
 (I like the stuff mixed with wild rice)

5 tbsp olive oil

1 onion, peeled and finely chopped

salt and pepper

50g/1³/₄oz flaked almonds, toasted

50g/1³/₄oz dried apricots, finely chopped

a good handful of fresh mint

a good handful of rocket (arugula),
 roughly chopped

juice of 1 lemon

AT HOME

Cook the rice according to packet instructions, then rinse under a cold tap until cool.

Meanwhile, heat a splash of oil in a small pan over a low heat and add the onion. Season with salt and pepper, and cook, stirring occasionally, until soft.

Stir the onions, almonds, apricot, mint, rocket, lemon juice and the remaining olive oil through the cooked rice. Taste for seasoning and adjust if necessary. Store in the fridge for up to 2 days.

IN EACH LUNCHBOX

A portion of rice salad.

TO FINISH

Eat.

GRIDDLED COURGETTE AND HALLOUMI SALAD WITH TOASTED QUINOA

Toasted quinoa is an excellent thing to have kicking about. Scattered over salads, tossed through pasta, or whatever, it adds a great nutty crunch to food. This particular recipe makes more than you need – it seemed to me that if you're going to toast quinoa, you may as well do more than a single tablespoon. Store it in a jar.

Prep time: 10 minutes

Cooking time: 25 minutes

Freezable? No

50g/1³/₄oz/¹/₃ cup quinoa

2 courgettes (zucchini), sliced thinly on
    the diagonal

2 tbsp olive oil

100g/3¹/₂oz halloumi cheese, cut into chunks

2 tbsp vegetable oil

salt and pepper

a good handful of rocket (arugula)

a few mint leaves, shredded

1 red chilli, deseeded and finely chopped

juice of ¹/₂ lemon

AT HOME

Boil the quinoa for 12 minutes, until tender. Drain and dry on kitchen paper as thoroughly as you can.

Meanwhile, heat a griddle or frying pan over a high heat. Toss the courgettes in 1 tbsp of the olive oil and griddle for a couple of minutes on each side. Remove the courgettes, add a little more olive oil and the halloumi, and cook for a minute on each side.

Heat the vegetable oil in a non-stick frying pan or sauté pan over a medium-high heat. Add the quinoa and a pinch of salt. Sauté, stirring occasionally, until golden, crisp and toasty, which should take 5 minutes. Set aside to cool.

Toss together the courgettes, halloumi, rocket, mint, chilli and lemon juice, and add a handful of toasted quinoa. Store in Tupperware in the fridge for up to 2 days.

IN EACH LUNCHBOX

A portion of courgette and halloumi salad.

TO FINISH

Eat.

Burnt leek and goat's cheese tart

I'm into burning alliums at the moment. Onions baked with sausages that have just caught slightly in the oven, spring onions charred, chopped, and stirred through sour cream, and leeks, aggressively griddled, hollowed out and stuffed with cheese and herbs. This is a sort of tartish interpretation of the latter dish.

You could replace the goat's cheese with goat's curd, but in the interests of speed use a soft goat's cheese.

Prep time: 25 minutes

Cooking time: 30 minutes

Freezable? Yes

200g/7oz puff pastry (shop-bought, obviously)

plain (all-purpose) flour for dusting

200g/7oz leeks, halved down the middle

100g/3¹/₂oz soft goat's cheese

1 egg, beaten

4 tbsp finely chopped parsley

2 tbsp finely chopped chives

salt and pepper

AT HOME

Preheat the oven to 160°C/325°F/Gas mark 3. Divide the pastry in half and roll out into rectangles the size of a paperback book. Prick a few times with a fork, place on a lightly floured baking sheet and chill.

Get a dry frying pan good and hot and add the leeks. Char for a few minutes on each side, until well blackened. Chop finely and beat together with the goat's cheese, most of the egg, and the herbs. Season generously.

Divide this mixture between the pastries, leaving a small border, and crimp around the edges. Brush the pastry with the remaining beaten egg and bake for 20–25 minutes. Leave to cool, cover and store in the fridge for up to 3 days.

IN EACH LUNCHBOX

A leek and goat's cheese tart.

TO FINISH

Serve cold, or reheat in an oven at 180°C/350°F/Gas mark 4 for 7 minutes.

PEA, SPRING ONION AND GRUYÈRE FRITTATA

The trick here is having a smallish frying pan (ideally a 16cm/6¼in omelette pan). If the frying pan's too wide, as Joni Mitchell discovered, then there's a risk of overcooking. It also means you don't get the benefit of a lovely fat frittata that's set top and bottom with a slightly wet middle.

Prep time: 10 minutes

Cooking time: 12 minutes

Freezable? No

1 tbsp olive oil

4 spring onions (scallions), roughly chopped

1 tsp finely chopped green chilli

salt and pepper

100g/3½oz/⅔ cup frozen peas

6 eggs, beaten vigorously

50g/1¾oz Gruyère cheese, grated

2 tbsp finely chopped parsley

AT HOME

Preheat the grill to high.

Heat the oil in a small frying pan over a medium heat and add the onions and chilli. Season with salt and pepper, and fry for a couple of minutes until softened, stirring occasionally.

Add the peas and shuggle the pan to separate them, then add the eggs, cheese and parsley. Add a little more salt and pepper, and cook over the lowest heat possible for 10 minutes, until set on the bottom but still runny on top.

Cook under the grill for 2 minutes, until set and a little browned. Leave to cool, then store in the fridge for up to 2 days.

IN EACH LUNCHBOX

Fat slices of frittata.

TO FINISH

Serve cold, with a green salad if you like.

CHAPTER 7
SANDWICHES

The sandwich is surely the quintessential midweek lunch, devoured and adored around the world, from the Franco-Vietnamese *banh mi* to the humble cheese and pickle, from the meatball sub to the endless permutations of the Scandi *smørrebrød*.

Helen Graves, queen of the sandwich as far as I'm concerned, and author of the comprehensive and sensational *101 Sandwiches*, explains it to me thus:
The insane popularity of the sandwich is surely owed to its convenience and versatility. A basic sarnie can be fashioned in minutes, but it's also good to put in a little extra effort occasionally. The world boasts some incredibly elaborate sandwich recipes, for example, the French-Viet mash-up that is the *banh mi* (a lesson in the power of contrasts), or the Portuguese *franceshina*, which packs four kinds of meat, cheese and, outrageously, beer sauce. How can you not instantly love anything that's drowned in beer sauce? There are endless combinations of fillings and wrappings to be explored but to be honest, for me, it's very hard to beat a well-cooked ham number with slightly too much nose-searing English mustard.

Can't argue with that, though you don't need me to give you a recipe for ham and mustard sandwiches. Here are 7 of my favourites.

CREAM CHEESE, SMOKED SALMON AND PICKLED CUCUMBER BAGEL

This is a handy recipe for when you've got leftover *labneh* (p.34) floating around, and indeed it's worth making a batch anyway, but failing that you can break out the cream cheese.

Bagels tend to be better when freshly toasted, which means assembling this at work, but do it in advance if you'd prefer.

Prep time: 10 minutes,
plus minimum 1 hour pickling
Freezable? No

2 bagels, halved
75g/2¾oz cream cheese or *labneh* (p.34)
100g/3½oz smoked salmon trimmings
salt and pepper
For the pickled cucumber
100g/3½oz/½ cup caster (superfine) sugar
150ml/5fl oz/⅔ cup white wine vinegar
a pinch of salt
½ cucumber, thinly sliced
1 shallot, peeled and thinly sliced

AT HOME
To make the pickled cucumber, whisk the sugar and vinegar with a pinch of salt, until dissolved. Tip over the cucumber and shallot in a jar or small bowl and leave for at least 1 hour. Store in the fridge.

IN EACH LUNCHBOX
A bagel; cream cheese; smoked salmon; cucumber pickle.

TO FINISH
Lightly toast the bagel. Slather the bottom half with cream cheese. Top with smoked salmon and season with salt and plenty of pepper. Finish with a spoonful of pickle and the other half of the bagel.

A SANDWICH OF DUBIOUSLY ITALIAN PROVENANCE

When I was 17, I did an Italian exchange to Liguria in north–west Italy. The family I stayed with was lovely and kind and generous and fed me like a soldier. Sending me off on a trip one day, the mother forced a packed lunch of quite extraordinary proportions on me, comprising, among other things, a trio of sandwiches that could each have dispatched a goose. Not wanting to be rude, I gobbled the lot, only to find my hostess lost for words at the gluttony of this strange English boy. I believe she was just trying to give me several options, though my Italian wasn't good enough to be sure.

This sanger is partly based on that sandwich and partly based on *muffuletta*, an Italo–Louisianian sandwich.

Prep time: 10 minutes

Freezable? No

200g/7oz focaccia bread

50g/1¾oz pitted green olives, finely chopped

2 tbsp finely chopped parsley

1 shallot, peeled and finely sliced

½ small garlic clove, peeled and finely chopped

1 tbsp olive oil

salt and pepper

slices of salami

slices of mortadella or other pinkishly
    cured sausage

100g/3½oz mozzarella or provolone cheese, sliced

AT HOME

Cut the focaccia in two and then halve each piece horizontally.

Mix the olives, parsley, shallot, garlic and olive oil. Season with salt and pepper, and spoon over the bottom half of each sandwich-to-be.

Top with salami, mortadella and cheese, add a twist of pepper and a drop of oil, if you like, and finish with the other piece of bread. Press down firmly, then wrap tightly in clingfilm and store in the fridge for up to a day.

IN EACH LUNCHBOX

A sandwich.

TO FINISH

Eat cold, or warm in an oven at 180°C/350°F/ Gas mark 4 for 10 minutes. Come to that, you could also pop it in a toastie maker.

PASTRAMI ON RYE

Food-porn-style versions of this tend to involve great hillocks of pastrami wedged inside a couple of floppy slices of bread, which is all well and good in some contexts but a bit impractical for the lunchy worky environment.

You need a soft rye bread as opposed to those sturdier Scandinavian varieties. You should be able to find one in your supermarket or certainly in a local, super-seasonal, crazy-organic baker.

I'd recommend assembling this at work so you can lightly toast the bread, but no matter if this isn't doable.

Prep time: 5 minutes

Cooking time: 2 minutes

4 slices of rye bread

softened butter

French's American mustard

about 75g/2¾oz sliced Emmental cheese

150g/5½oz pastrami, sliced

4 gherkins, thinly sliced, or 4 tbsp sauerkraut

salt and pepper

If assembling at work, lightly toast the bread. If not, don't.

Lavishly butter two pieces of bread/toast, then spread with mustard. Top with Emmental, then pastrami, then gherkins. Season with salt and pepper and a hefty squirt of mustard. Top with the other slice of bread and press down enthusiastically. Eat forthwith, or wrap tightly in clingfilm and store somewhere out of harm's way until lunchtime.

THREE–CHEESE TOASTIE WITH SPINACH AND CHILLI JAM

Toasties seem to have had a bit of a fall from grace for some reason, which is a shame. I love 'em, and while the toastie machine is a little cumbersome, it's more versatile than you might think. You can cook bacon on it.

Should you or your office not be the proud owner of a toastie maker, however, then you can grill the cheese and top with a slice of lightly toasted bread, or toast in a frying pan. Worst comes to worst, just eat it as a three–cheese sandwich.

Prep time: 10 minutes

Cooking time: 5 minutes

4 slices of bread

2 tbsp chilli jam

a handful of spinach leaves or rocket (arugula)

50g/1³⁄₄oz Taleggio cheese, sliced

50g/1³⁄₄oz Gorgonzola cheese, crumbled

50g/1³⁄₄oz mozzarella cheese, sliced

salt and pepper

AT HOME

Spread two of the slices of bread with the chilli jam.

Top with spinach leaves and then the cheeses.

Season with pepper and a little salt. Finish with the remaining slices of bread and press down. Wrap tightly in clingfilm and refrigerate if necessary.

IN EACH LUNCHBOX

A cheese sandwich.

TO FINISH

Toast in a toastie maker. Otherwise, heat a little oil in a non-stick frying pan over a medium-high heat and toast for 2 minutes on each side.

Vietnamese baguette (banh mi)

This is fusion food at its finest, a marriage of French ingredients with Vietnamese, hailing from the French colonial rule of Vietnam. Serve warm if possible.

Prep time: 15 minutes,
 plus minimum 1 hour pickling

2 small baguettes
2 tbsp mayonnaise
85g/3oz country pâté
150g/5$^{1}/_{2}$oz cooked pork belly, sliced
$^{1}/_{2}$ cucumber, peeled, deseeded, and cut
 into matchsticks
$^{1}/_{2}$ red chilli, deseeded and thinly sliced
20g/$^{3}/_{4}$oz coriander (cilantro), leaves only
salt and pepper

For the pickled carrot
100ml/3$^{1}/_{2}$fl oz/scant $^{1}/_{2}$ cup rice vinegar
2 tbsp caster (superfine) sugar
$^{1}/_{2}$ tsp salt
1 small carrot, peeled and cut into thin
 matchsticks, or grated
$^{1}/_{2}$ red onion, finely sliced

AT HOME

First make the pickled carrot: mix the vinegar, sugar and salt together until the sugar has dissolved, then mix in the carrot and onion. Leave for at least 1 hour.

Slice open the baguettes and spread each one generously with mayonnaise and pâté. Fill with slices of pork belly, cucumber, chilli and coriander.

Drain the pickled carrot and add this to the baguettes. Season with salt and pepper, wrap tightly in foil or clingfilm and refrigerate for up to a day.

IN EACH LUNCHBOX

A banh mi.

TO FINISH

Eat cold if you prefer/have no option, or wrap in foil and warm in an oven at 180°C/350°F/Gas mark 4 for 10 minutes.

SLOW-COOKED BEEF BUNS WITH SMOKED CHILLI SOUR CREAM

You could use up leftover beef stew to make this sandwich, though you can just as easily cook the beef specially, as here.

Chipotle chillies are smoked jalapeños, which you can find increasingly in the supermarket, or order online. Alternatively, use chipotle paste, or smoked paprika.

Prep time: 15 minutes
Cooking time: 2 hours

olive oil
300g/10¹/₂oz beef shin or other slow-cooking cut,
    cut into chunks
salt and pepper
300ml/10fl oz/1¹/₄ cups beef stock
a splash of beer (optional)
1 tbsp tomato purée (tomato paste)
1 dried red chilli
1 chipotle chilli, or 1 tsp hot smoked paprika or
    chipotle paste
2 tbsp sour cream
juice of ¹/₂ lime
2 crusty buns
1 Little Gem lettuce, shredded
a good handful of coriander (cilantro)

AT HOME

Heat a little oil in a saucepan and brown the beef all over, seasoning with salt and pepper. Add the beef stock, beer (if using), tomato purée and dried chilli and bring to a boil. Simmer for a minute or two, then cover and cook for 1¹/₂–2 hours over a low heat, stirring every now and then. Once tender, rest for 10 minutes, then shred the meat with a pair of forks. Cool.

Meanwhile, boil the kettle and pour over the chipotle chilli, if using. Leave for 10 minutes, then chop finely. Stir through the sour cream, along with the lime juice.

Pack the buns with the cooled beef and lather with the spicy sour cream. Finish with shredded lettuce and coriander. Wrap tightly in clingfilm and store in the fridge for up to a day.

IN EACH LUNCHBOX
A beef bun.

TO FINISH
Eat.

SPICED LAMB WRAP

Another one of those recipes that are a good use of leftover meat, though I thoroughly recommend making this specially.

Prep time: 15 minutes

Cooking time: 3 minutes

150g/5½oz lamb leg steaks, trimmed, or
  150g/5½oz leftover lamb, thinly sliced

1 tsp grated fresh ginger

½ tsp grated garlic

2 tsp finely chopped green chilli

½ tsp ground cumin

1 tsp garam masala

a squeeze of lemon juice

salt and pepper

1 tbsp vegetable oil

2 tbsp plain yogurt

1 tbsp mango chutney

2 rotis, tortillas or pittas

1 Little Gem lettuce, sliced

1 tomato, chopped

½ red onion, very finely sliced

a good handful of coriander (cilantro)

AT HOME

Mix the lamb, ginger, garlic, chilli, cumin, garam masala and lemon juice. Season with a pinch of salt and leave for as long as you can.

In a hot pan, heat the oil and fry the spiced lamb slices for about a minute on each side. Remove to a plate.

Mix the yogurt and mango chutney and spread over the breads. Top with the lettuce, tomato and onion, then the lamb and finally the coriander. Wrap tightly and eat, or wrap again in foil and refrigerate for up to a day.

IN EACH LUNCHBOX

A lamb wrap.

TO FINISH

Eat cold, or reheat in an oven at 180°C/350°F/ Gas mark 4 for 7–10 minutes.

CHAPTER 8
FRUGAL

A chapter for those long days at the end of the month when you find yourself counting the hours until payday. The temptation to live off Ryvita and margarine can be irresistible, though for a little more lucre and a mite more effort you can eat handsomely without spending much more than a couple of quid on your lunch.

Canned food is often a good place to start, though isn't necessarily where the bargains end. Those little red labels on nearly out-of-date products are a handy guide (unlike spurious 3 for 2 offers), just as hitting the supermarket 15 minutes before closing often yields some heavily discounted meat and fish.

Ultimately, as you already know, you can eat very well for very little, even if the menu is somewhat restricted.

Swedish Meatballs

Not a bad idea to make several times the amount of meatballs here, to store in the freezer – very handy things to have on an Empty Fridge Night.

Serve with a green salad and some crusty bread, or some of that microwaveable rice.

Prep time: 15 minutes, plus chilling

Cooking time: 25 minutes

Freezable? Yes

300g/10½oz fresh minced (ground) pork

25g/1oz/¼ cup dried breadcrumbs

1 egg

½ tsp ground allspice

1 tbsp finely chopped dill, plus extra to garnish

salt and pepper

olive oil

1 small onion, peeled and finely chopped

100ml/3½fl oz/scant ½ cup double (heavy) cream

100ml/3½fl oz/scant ½ cup chicken stock or water

2 tbsp cranberry sauce

AT HOME

Mix the pork, breadcrumbs, egg, allspice and dill, adding a good pinch of salt and twist of pepper. Form into 10–12 meatballs and chill in the fridge for 30 minutes, or freezer for 10 minutes.

Heat a little oil in a sauté or frying pan over a medium–low heat and cook the onion until soft. Add the meatballs and continue to cook over a medium heat, turning every now and then and stirring the onion, until crisp on the outside. Add the cream, stock and cranberry sauce and cook for a further 10 minutes. Leave to cool. Store in the fridge for up to 2 days.

IN EACH LUNCHBOX

Portion of meatballs (in a microwaveable vessel); accompaniment of your choice (crusty bread, rice, salad).

TO FINISH

Reheat the meatballs in a microwave on medium for 4–5 minutes.

Sticky rice with spiced cabbage and chicken wings

This was inspired by a dish at Bruno Loubet's terrific restaurant Grain Store, where the whole thing comes in a lotus leaf, its wings stuffed and its cabbage properly fermented. I – and I imagine you – don't have the time nor the inclination, midweek at least, to start stuffing chicken wings, so this is a simplified interpretation.

Prep time: 15 minutes

Cooking time: 1 hour

Freezable? No

1 tbsp rice vinegar

1 tbsp soy sauce

1 litre/1³/₄ pints/4 cups chicken stock or water

4 chicken wings

salt and pepper

100g/3¹/₂oz/¹/₂ cup short-grain rice

For the cabbage

1 tbsp vegetable oil

4 spring onions (scallions), roughly chopped

1 garlic clove, peeled and thinly sliced

2 tsp grated fresh ginger

¹/₂ tsp hot chilli powder

1 tbsp Thai fish sauce

150g/5¹/₂oz white or Chinese cabbage, roughly chopped

1 tsp salt

AT HOME

For the cabbage: heat the oil in a large frying pan or wok over a medium-high heat. Add the spring onions, garlic and ginger, and stir for 30 seconds, then add the chilli powder, fish sauce, cabbage and salt. Stir-fry for 2–3 minutes, then transfer to a bowl and set aside.

Put the rice vinegar, soy sauce and stock in a saucepan. Bring to a boil and add the chicken wings, along with a pinch of salt. Cover and gently poach for 45 minutes, then remove the wings and cool.

Bring 200ml/7fl oz/generous ³/₄ cup of the cooking liquor back to a boil and add the rice. Cover and cook over a low heat for 15 minutes, then take off the heat and leave for another 15 minutes. Tip onto a baking sheet to cool.

Pull all the meat off the cooled chicken wings and combine with the rice and the cabbage. Season, and store in the fridge for up to 2 days.

IN EACH LUNCHBOX

Sticky rice, chicken and cabbage (in a microwaveable vessel).

TO FINISH

Reheat in a microwave on medium for 4–5 minutes.

Ham hock, beans and cider

A pig's hock is essentially its ankle, which you probably could work out just by looking at the thing. The piggy equivalent of a lamb shank, this is similarly best when slowly cooked until it comes off the bone. But this is a cheat's recipe, and uses already cooked ham hock, which you can often find in large supermarkets. If this isn't doable, use sausage instead.

Prep time: 15 minutes

Cooking time: 20 minutes
    (55 minutes if using sausage)

Freezable? Yes

olive oil

1 onion, peeled and roughly chopped

1 garlic clove, peeled and roughly chopped

1 celery stalk, roughly chopped

salt and pepper

150g/5½oz cooked ham hock, or
    2–4 sausages, cut into chunks

200ml/7fl oz/generous ¾ cup dry cider

400ml/14fl oz/1 ⅔ cups chicken or ham stock

1 x 400g/14oz can butter beans (lima beans),
    drained and rinsed

1 tbsp tomato purée (tomato paste)

1 bay leaf

a handful of parsley, roughly chopped

AT HOME

Heat a little oil in a saucepan and add the onion, garlic and celery. Season with salt and pepper, and cook gently for 10 minutes or so, stirring often.

Add the ham hock or sausages, cider, stock, beans, tomato purée and bay leaf, and stir to combine.

Bring to a boil and simmer, uncovered, for 10 minutes (45 minutes if using sausages).

Leave to cool, then store in the fridge for up to 2 days.

IN EACH LUNCHBOX

A portion of ham hock and beans (in a microwaveable vessel); chopped parsley.

TO FINISH

Reheat in a microwave on medium for 4–5 minutes. Sprinkle with parsley and serve.

CORONATION CHICKPEAS

A bit of lunchtime retro.

Prep time: 15 minutes

Cooking time: 20 minutes

Freezable? Yes

a small knob of butter

1 onion, peeled and finely chopped

1 garlic clove, peeled and finely chopped

1/2 green chilli, deseeded and finely chopped

salt and pepper

5 cardamom pods

1 tbsp mild curry powder

1/4 tsp turmeric

2 x 400g/14oz cans chickpeas, drained and rinsed

150g/5^{1}/$_{2}$oz/^{2}/$_{3}$ cup plain yogurt

1 generous tbsp mango chutney

a handful of coriander (cilantro)

naan bread, roti or pitta, to serve

AT HOME

Melt the butter in a saucepan over a low heat and add the onion, garlic and chilli. Season with salt and pepper, cover, and cook for 10 minutes, until soft.

Add the spices and stir over a medium heat for a minute, then add the chickpeas and a splash of water. Cover and cook for 10 minutes, then leave to cool.

Stir through the yogurt and mango chutney. Taste for seasoning. Roughly chop the coriander and mix through. Store in the fridge for up to 3 days.

IN EACH LUNCHBOX

A portion of coronation chickpeas; naan bread, roti or pitta.

TO FINISH

Gently warm the bread, if you prefer, and serve with the chickpeas.

SPICY CHICKEN SALAD

This is based on a south-east Asian salad, *larb gai*, which is, like much of the food in them parts, pretty fiery. This is a pared-back version, though you could always ramp up the chilli quotient. Should keep your colleagues off your lunch, if nothing else.

Prep time: 20 minutes
Cooking time: 7 minutes
Freezable? Yes

2–3 skinless, boneless chicken thighs
1 shallot, peeled and chopped
stalks from a bunch of coriander (cilantro),
    finely chopped
1/2 stalk of lemongrass, finely chopped
zest of 1/2 lime
1 red chilli, deseeded and finely chopped
1 tbsp Thai fish sauce
1 tbsp groundnut (peanut) or vegetable oil, plus
    extra for cooking
4 large-ish Little Gem lettuce leaves (outer leaves,
    as opposed to inner)
coriander (cilantro) leaves

For the dressing
juice of 1/2 lime
1 tbsp Thai fish sauce
1 tsp soft brown sugar
bottom half of a Thai chilli, finely chopped

AT HOME

Put the chicken, shallot, coriander stalks, lemongrass, lime zest, chilli, fish sauce and 1 tbsp oil in a blender and pulse until the chicken is well minced. Alternatively, finely and thoroughly chop with a knife.

Heat a splash of oil in a sauté pan or saucepan over a medium-high heat and add the chicken mixture. Cook, stirring regularly, for about 7 minutes, until cooked through and crisp in places. Set aside to cool, then store in the fridge for up to 2 days.

Mix the dressing ingredients together and store in a jar.

IN EACH LUNCHBOX

A portion of chicken (in a microwaveable vessel); lettuce leaves, coriander; dressing.

TO FINISH

Reheat the chicken in a microwave on medium for 3–4 minutes. Serve on lettuce leaves with a few coriander leaves and a spoonful of dressing.

Miʃo ʃoup with a boiled egg

This is clean, nourishing simplicity. If you have spent the morning tilling the earth, carrying heavy machinery, or on an interminable conference call, it may not cut the mustard. But if it's an inactive day and perhaps you're doing a diet that involves eating a modest lunch, this is the one for you. Should you want to bulk it up, bung in some noodles, chopped spring onion and leftover chicken.

Prep time: 5 minutes

Cooking time: 5 minutes

Freezable? You could in theory freeze the miso soup, but seeing as it comes in a sachet I'm not sure why you would need to

2 eggs

2 sachets of instant miso soup paste

Sriracha hot sauce (optional)

AT HOME

Bring a pan of water to a boil. Slide in the eggs and boil for 5 minutes. Remove with a slotted spoon and dunk into a bowl of cold water until cool. Peel and store in a small container in the fridge.

IN EACH LUNCHBOX

A boiled egg; miso sachet; hot sauce (optional).

TO FINISH

Boil a kettle. Put the miso sachet and the egg in a bowl or large mug. Tip over boiling water, stir, and leave to stand for 1 minute. Eat with Sriracha sauce if you like.

SWEET POTATO AND LENTIL CURRY

SERVES 2

As with other spiced dishes in this book, I realize there is a risk of creating office tensions, as the waft of the orient drifts across computer screens and up nostrils. Homemade jaffa cakes (p.120) should resolve matters.

Prep time: 15 minutes

Cooking time: 35 minutes

Freezable? Yes

vegetable oil

1 red onion, peeled and sliced

1 garlic clove, peeled and thinly sliced

2 tsp grated fresh ginger

salt and pepper

1 tsp onion seeds (optional)

1 tbsp garam masala

100g/3^1/$_2$oz/^{1}/$_2$ cup red lentils, rinsed

1 large sweet potato, cubed

200ml/7fl oz/generous ^{3}/$_4$ cup coconut milk

1 tbsp tomato purée (tomato paste)

200ml/7fl oz/generous ^{3}/$_4$ cup water or stock

To serve

naan bread or roti (or pitta)

plain yogurt

coriander (cilantro) leaves

AT HOME

Heat a little oil in a saucepan over a medium heat and add the onion, garlic and ginger. Season with salt and pepper, and cook for about 7 minutes, stirring regularly, until softened.

Add the spices and stir for a minute or so, then add the lentils, sweet potato, coconut milk, tomato purée and water. Give it a good stir and bring to a boil. Cover and simmer gently for 25 minutes, stirring occasionally, until the lentils are tender and breaking up. Cool and store in the fridge for up to 3 days.

IN EACH LUNCHBOX

Portion of curry (in a microwaveable vessel); bread; yogurt; fresh coriander.

TO FINISH

Reheat in a microwave on medium for 4–5 minutes. Warm some bread. Serve with a dollop of yogurt and a few coriander leaves.

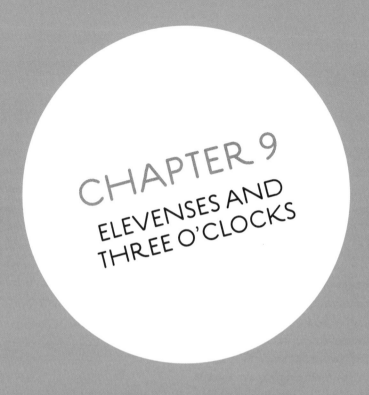

CHAPTER 9
ELEVENSES AND THREE O'CLOCKS

Those long mornings and even longer afternoons, those meetings in which not even an elaborate torture mechanism could keep you awake, the excruciating feeling of nodding off only to realize you've missed some crucial nugget of information, are made all the easier by having something to nibble on during the slump. It lifts the spirits and provides a bit of zip to see you through the rest of the day.

The idea that these ought to be unhealthy or even guilt-tinged is misguided – they can be a little naughty, but they can also be relatively virtuous. Eating between meals is not the shameful submission it's made out to be. There's nothing wrong with a piece of cake with your afternoon cup of tea. Two pieces of cake with every cup of tea and there's a problem...

Oatcakes

I've been making these for years now and adore them. You can muck about with what goes in them, sweetening them if you wish, or adding different flavours and textures (snipped chives, for example), though here I've opted for the straightforward version.

Eat with butter and honey.

Prep time: 15 minutes, plus 15 minutes resting

Cooking time: 20 minutes

Freezable? Yes

200g/7oz medium oatmeal

50g/1³/₄oz/7 tbsp wholemeal flour

¹/₂ tsp salt

¹/₂ tsp bicarbonate of soda (baking soda)

50g/1³/₄oz/4 tbsp butter, softened

50–70ml/about 2fl oz/4–5 tbsp hot water from the kettle

freshly ground pepper

plain (all-purpose) flour for dusting

AT HOME

Preheat the oven to 180°C/350°F/Gas mark 4.

Mix the oatmeal, flour, salt and bicarb, then add the butter and rub together with your palms (use a blender if you prefer) to form even crumbs. Add the hot water and a few twists of pepper, and mix until it comes together to form a dense dough. Add more water if necessary, or a little flour if too wet. Cover with a tea towel and leave to rest for 15 minutes.

Lightly flour a work surface and a baking sheet. Roll out the dough to about 5mm/¹/₄in thick. Cut into oatcakes (I tend to go for triangles) and transfer to the floured baking sheet.

Bake for 15–20 minutes, until starting to colour. Cool on a wire rack, and store in a tin for up to 2 weeks.

RYE CRISPBREADS

You'll no doubt be familiar with the leading brand when it comes to rye crispbreads, but it's incredibly easy to make your own, and they do, of course, taste better.

Prep time: 10 minutes, plus 30 minutes resting

Cooking time: 25 minutes

Freezable? Yes

200g/7oz/generous 1¹/₂ cups rye flour

100g/3¹/₂oz/generous ³/₄ cup plain (all-purpose) flour, plus extra for dusting

7g/¹/₄oz/about 1 tsp fast-action dried yeast

¹/₂ tsp salt

a few twists of the pepper mill

250ml/9fl oz/1 cup warm water

Preheat the oven to 180°C/350°F/Gas mark 4.

Mix all the ingredients together, then knead on a lightly floured surface for a couple of minutes until smooth. Cover with a tea towel and leave to rest for 30 minutes.

Lightly flour a work surface and a baking sheet. Roll out the dough as thinly as you can. Prick a few times with a fork, and cut into squares. Transfer to the floured baking sheet.

Bake for 20–25 minutes. Cool on a wire rack, and store in a tin for up to 2 weeks.

Honey and cardamom popcorn

It probably goes without saying that this stuff is terrific eaten hot, in front of a film, but it's just as decent munched cold.

Prep time: 5 minutes

Cooking time: 10 minutes

Freezable? No

2 tbsp unsalted butter

4 tbsp runny honey

seeds from 5 cardamom pods, lightly crushed

a pinch of salt

1 tbsp vegetable oil

100g/3½oz popping corn (unpopped kernels)

Melt the butter in a small pan and add the honey, cardamom seeds and salt. Simmer over a medium heat for a few minutes, then set aside.

Heat the oil in a large pan over a medium heat. Add the popcorn, cover and shake, then turn up the heat to medium–high. Keep cooking, shaking the pan regularly, until the pops start to subside. Take off the heat and leave for a couple of minutes.

Drizzle over the honey mixture and give it a good shake. Leave to cool. Store in a sandwich bag or similar.

HOMEMADE JAFFA CAKES

MAKES 12

In all honesty, I worried this recipe might be too gimmicky and unnecessary: after all, a shop-bought jaffa cake is a fine thing. But this is worth the effort, and far better than anything from a packet.

Prep time: 30 minutes, plus chilling

Cooking time: 30 minutes

Freezable? Yes

150g/5½oz/generous ½ cup butter, softened, plus extra for greasing

150g/5½oz/¾ cup caster (superfine) sugar

2 large eggs, beaten

½ tsp vanilla extract

150g/5½oz/1¼ cups self-raising flour

a pinch of salt

For the orange jelly

vegetable oil for greasing

juice of 2 oranges

juice of 1 lemon

100g/3½oz/½ cup caster (superfine) sugar

3 leaves of gelatine, soaked in cold water until soft

For the chocolate

100g/3½oz dark chocolate, broken into pieces

Preheat the oven to 180°C/350°F/Gas mark 4. Grease a 12-hole muffin tin.

Beat together the butter and sugar until pale and fluffy, then, a little at a time, beat in the eggs. Add the vanilla, then fold in the flour and salt. Spoon into the muffin tin and bake for 18–20 minutes. Leave to cool completely on a wire rack, then chill.

Lightly brush a small baking sheet with vegetable oil and chill in the freezer for at least 15 minutes.

To make the jelly: bring the orange and lemon juice to a boil with the sugar, stirring to dissolve. Simmer for 5 minutes. Squeeze the moisture out of the gelatine and add to the juice. Stir to dissolve the gelatine, then tip onto the chilled baking sheet. You want a thickness of about 5mm/¼in. Chill in the fridge for 30 minutes to 1 hour, until set.

Using a cookie cutter, or a mug and a knife, cut rounds of the jelly slightly smaller than the top of the muffins, and lay on top. Put them back in the fridge.

Melt the chocolate in a heatproof bowl over a pan of barely simmering water, stir until smooth and glossy, then leave to cool until slightly thickened but still pourable. Spoon over the muffins. Cool in the fridge until set; enjoy with a cup of tea.

ORANGE, YOGURT AND
PISTACHIO CAKE

I do enjoy using yogurt instead of butter in cakes. It adds a nice touch of sourness, as well as a slightly stickier texture. If you want something more cakey, as opposed to puddingy, you can omit the syrup part of this recipe.

Prep time: 15 minutes

Cooking time: 45 minutes

Freezable? Yes

vegetable oil, for greasing

3 eggs, plus 1 egg yolk

225g/8oz/generous 1 cup caster (superfine) sugar

225g/8oz/1¾ cups self-raising flour

225g/8oz/scant 1 cup plain yogurt

zest of 1 orange

zest of ½ lemon

50g/1¾oz pistachios, finely chopped, plus
  a few to garnish

a pinch of salt

For the syrup (optional)

juice of 1 orange

juice of ½ lemon

50g/1¾oz/¼ cup caster (superfine) sugar

1 clove

Preheat the oven to 180°C/350°F/Gas mark 4. Line the bottom of a 20cm/8in round cake tin with baking parchment, and grease the sides with a little oil.

Whisk together the eggs, yolk and sugar until pale and light. Fold in the flour, then the yogurt, zest, pistachios and salt. Decant into the prepared cake tin and bake for 45 minutes. If it starts to colour on top, cover with a little foil.

For the syrup, put the orange and lemon juice in a saucepan with the sugar and clove. Bring to a boil, stirring to dissolve the sugar, and simmer for 3 minutes. Remove from the heat.

When the cake is cooked and still warm, pierce with a skewer a few times and tip over the syrup. Leave to cool, then carefully turn out. Garnish with pistachios if you like. Wrap in foil and store in a Tupperware in the fridge for up to a week.